387.243   c.2
N4o
NEWELL
OCEAN LINERS OF THE 20TH CENTURY

23817
3.98

DATE DUE			
MAY 24 '82			
JAN 3 '83			
FEB 25 '88			
APR 14 '89			
ILL Fueston			
2/21/91			

College of the Siskiyous Library
Weed, California

S.S. ROTTERDAM
(HOLLAND-AMERICA LINE)

OCEAN LINERS
of the 20th Century

OCEAN L

NERS *of the* 20th *Century*
by Gordon Newell

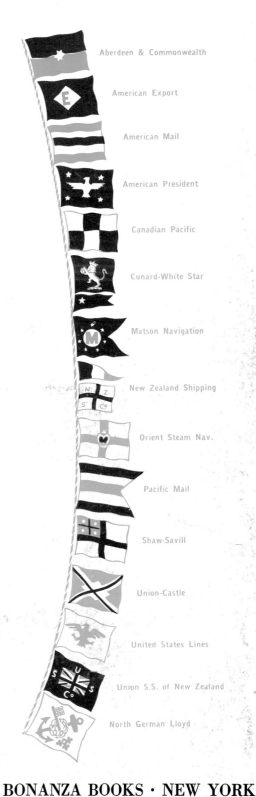

Aberdeen & Commonwealth

American Export

American Mail

American President

Canadian Pacific

Cunard-White Star

Matson Navigation

New Zealand Shipping

Orient Steam Nav.

Pacific Mail

Shaw-Savill

Union-Castle

United States Lines

Union S.S. of New Zealand

North German Lloyd

BONANZA BOOKS · NEW YORK

MAURETANIA in World War I

517 03168X
Copyright © MCMLXIII by Superior Publishing Company
Library Of Congress Catalog Card Number: 63-18484
All rights reserved.
This edition is published by Bonanza Books
a division of Crown Publishers, Inc.
by arrangement with Superior Publishing Company
c d e f g h
Manufactured in the United States Of America

Dedicated to
Horace Winslow McCurdy
Builder of Ships
Lover of the Sea
Gentleman

ACKNOWLEDGEMENTS

The kind assistance of the following firms and individuals in providing pictorial material and information for this book is deeply appreciated: H. T. Coleman and Canadian Pacific Steamships Ltd., Tom Wheeler and American President Lines, Charles Regal and Matson Navigation Co., Carl W. Hallengren and Swedish American Line, William B. Saphire and Zim Israel Shipping Co., Miss B. A. Perkins and Union-Castle Mail Steamship Co., Ltd., George V. Bigelow and the Cunard Steamship Co., Ltd., Arthur H. Richter and Home Lines Agency Inc., Jan H. Westerman and Holland-America Line, James P. McDonald and United States Lines, Howard A. Schrieffer and Delta Steamship Lines, Inc., Charles J. Hogan and the French Line, Warren S. Titus, Deborah Ogden and P & O-Orient Lines Inc., V. Rollo and the Italian Line, Howard S. Kennedy and Moore-McCormack Lines, W. Collier and Shaw Savill Line, Merle Macbain and Caribbean News Bureau, Frank O. Braynard and Moran Towing & Transportation Co., Inc., Brad Mitchell and the American Merchant Marine Institute, Mrs. Alice S. Wilson and the Steamship Historical Society of America, Inc., The Puget Sound Bridge & Dry Dock Co. and Lockheed Aviation Corporation, The Seattle Historical Society, Lee K. Jaffe and Port of New York Authority, and the British National Maritime Museum, Greenwich.

FORWORD

This fifth in the Superior series of maritime picture books is the first to sail "deep-water" beyond the regional confines of the coastal and inland waters of the Pacific Coast.

As in previous books of the series, there are a number of things this volume does *not* attempt to do. It does not pretend to cover all the many hundreds of passenger carrying steam and motor ships which have sailed the world's considerably more than seven seas since the turn of the century. Being designed for the general reader, it does not contain the mass of facts, figures and statistical material dear to the heart of the dedicated maritime enthusiast. And, finally, it does not claim to be infallible. The writer has been taken to task on previous occasions by scholarly maritime publications whose reviewers are not in agreement with my theory that books entirely without errors take so long to get written that they seldom get printed. While a reasonable effort toward accuracy has been made, I will not beat my head against the wall in anguish if somebody confronts me with the awful fact that the S. S. *Tokumoto Maru* was really launched in 1910 rather than 1911 and carried 659 passengers rather than 650.

There are in print several reference books about ocean liners of a comprehensiveness and accuracy almost superhuman. If they say the *Tokumoto Maru* was launched in 1910 rather than 1911 we'll concede in advance, they are doubtless right and we are wrong; 1910 it was.

What this book *does* try to do is impart a bit of the glamor, the majesty and the color of the most exciting things ever built by man . . . the Ocean Liners.

Representative ships of the world's major liner routes are covered in picture and text, along with reproductions of what antique book fanciers call "ephemera" . . . menues from the salons, posters, sailing schedules, deck plans and souvenir programs. Brief histories of most of the major shipping companies presently operating passenger liners are included. And there's a salting of assorted sea yarns thrown in because I like them and hope my readers will.

If this book leaves the reader with a memory of a lean, rakish *schnelldampfer* of the old German Lloyd rolling down the North Atlantic road with the coal-smoke pouring from her four tall stacks, or of the great *Queen Mary* flinging her majestic challenge to all the air and sea forces of her country's enemies, or the poignant notes of a sailors' hymn as the requiem at the awesome death of *Titanic* off the Grand Banks of Newfoundland, then it has served its purpose.

TWIN-SCREW coal burning Red Star Liner **Lapland** of 1908 was typical early twentieth century trans-Atlantic steamer.

Much of the background material for this book was provided over the years by Ralph E. Cropley whose lifetime of deep devotion to ships and the sea ended in 1960. With a friend named Franklin Roosevelt, he was known to skip classes at Harvard to watch the ships come in at East Boston. Later he abandoned a banking career to ship out as purser on the old *President Arthur* in 1920. Retired as chief purser on Atlantic liners, he came to the West Coast to do his bit in the Korean emergency, his last service at sea being aboard the *Marine Phoenix*. He was then well past sixty-five. His many memorials include the Cropley maritime historical collection at the Smithsonian Institute and the International Model Collection at the Seamen's Church Institute, New York, where he was assistant curator and historian during the last five years of his life.

His last wish, that his ashes be scattered at sea in the Gulf Stream, was carried out by the master of the Peninsula & Occidental Liner *Florida*, one of "Doc" Cropley's favorite ships.

A bit of his sea lore lives on in this book, as it does, from Coast to Coast, wherever memories of ships and sailormen are cherished.

Finally let it be said, for every great and gallant ship whose story has been told here, there are a hundred that have been left out. I hope to write about some of them in another book of this series. If you find that your favorite ocean liner has been neglected, please let me hear from you. We'll try to find mooring-space for her in the next book of ships.

Gordon Newell
Seattle, Washington
June, 1963

TABLE OF CONTENTS

Color plate: S.S. *America*, foreground, and
S.S. *United States*, United States Lines, passing in New York Harbor.

. . . photo courtesy United States Lines

THE ADMIRAL LINE

PASSENGER ACCOMMODATION PLAN
S. S. PRESIDENT McKINLEY

LENGTH 535 FEET, BREADTH 72 FEET, DISPLACEMENT TONNAGE 21,000

BERTHING

FIRST CABIN

BRIDGE DECK	SUITES	2 { BEDS	4
		{ BERTHS	4
"A" DECK	ROOMS	31 BEDS AND BERTHS	83
"B" DECK—FORWARD	ROOMS	12 BEDS	24
"B" DECK—AMIDSHIP	ROOMS—OUTSIDE	3 BEDS	6
"B" DECK—AFT	ROOMS—OUTSIDE	22 BERTHS	77
TOTAL FIRST CABIN			198

STEERAGE

"B" DECK	BERTHS	138
"C" DECK	BERTHS	412
TOTAL STEERAGE		550

748

THE ADMIRAL LINE
PACIFIC STEAMSHIP COMPANY
MANAGING AGENTS
UNITED STATES SHIPPING BOARD
EMERGENCY FLEET CORPORATION
GENERAL OFFICES, L. C. SMITH BUILDING
SEATTLE, WASH.

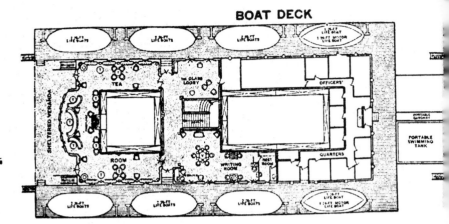

BOAT DECK

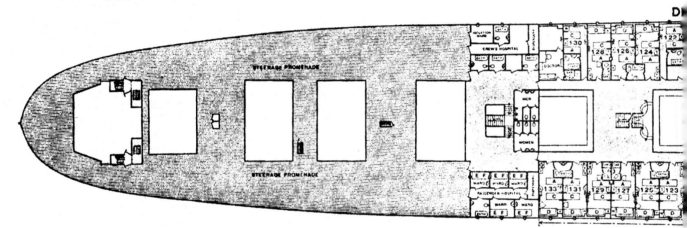

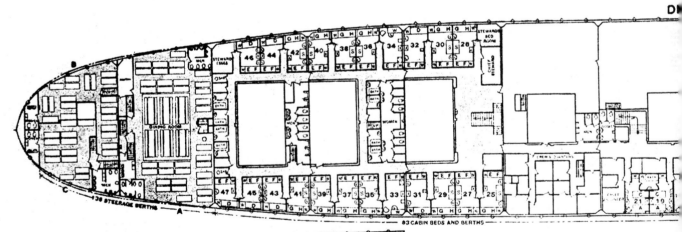

DECK C

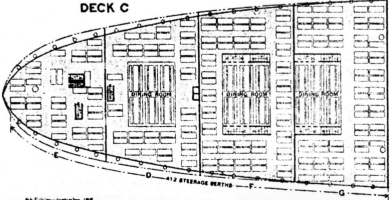

EXPLANATION
OF REFERENCE MARKS

AB		BEDS
C		FOLDING BED
D		SOFA BERTH
E		UPPER BERTH
F		LOWER BERTH
L		LAVATORY
S		SOFA SEAT
T		TABLE
V		WRITING TABLE

W——
X——
Y——
Z——
○ SHR

NOTE—ALL TUB BATHS ARE FITTED WITH NE
ROOMS ARE FITTED WITH ELECTRIC HEATER

TRANS-PACIFIC SERVICE

BRIDGE DECK

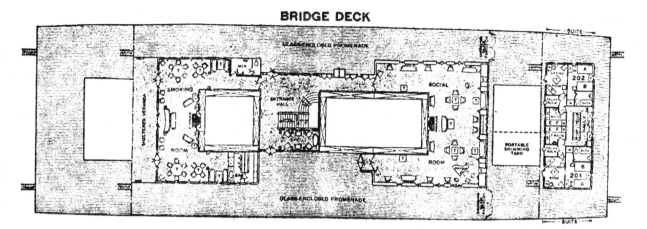

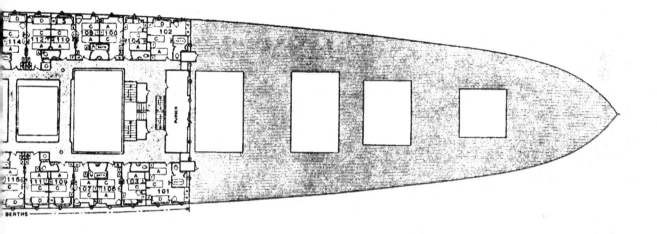

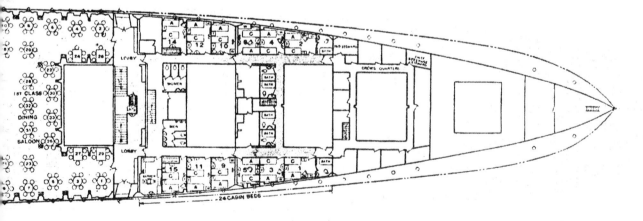

Chapter One
BLUE RIBAND

The Blue Riband of the Atlantic, the British call it. To Americans it's the *Blue Ribbon*, to the French, *Ruban Bleu*, to the Germans *Blau Band*. Whatever you call it, it's the symbol of the ultimate royalty of the sisterhood of the sea . . . the great racing liners of the North Atlantic. And in whatever language the phrase is spoken, it is one to stir the imagination of those who love ships and the sea.

The pride of the great maritime nations is involved in the winning of the Blue Riband. Fortunes have been invested, won and lost, and famous steamship lines have been created and destroyed in the battle for the pennant which can be flown only by the fastest passenger liner in the world.

During the first half of the nineteenth century the trans-Atlantic speed records were held by British and American steamships built of wood and driven by paddle-wheels. The fastest of them, the Collins Liner *Adriatic*, could maintain a sea speed of 13½ knots.

The second half of the nineteenth century was an era of transition on the sea-road of the trans-Atlantic racing liners. Single-screw iron ships like Cunard's *Scotia* of 1862, White Star's *Britannic* of 1874 and the Guion Liner *Oregon* of 1883 kept pushing the speed of the Riband Winners to eighteen knots and more.

With the coming of the Inman Line's *City of Paris*, first of the steel-hulled, twin-screw express liners, in 1889, the winning speed jumped above twenty knots. From then until the closing years of the century, the Blue Riband of the Atlantic was virtually monopolized by the British lines; *Teutonic*, White Star Line, averaged 20.35 knots to make the crossing in five days, 16 hours and 31 minutes in August, 1891. Cunard's *Campania* averaged 21.12 knots on her fastest crossing, in June of 1893. Her sister, *Lucania*, upped the average to an even 22 knots in May of 1895, holding the Blue Riband for more than two years.

Germany, emerging as a major maritime power, had yet to give serious competition to the racing liners of the British and American companies, but the German lines had been quietly improving their ships

and service while the Cunard, Inman and White Star lines were getting the headlines with their Riband-winning racers. In 1897 Germany served notice that she was entering the competition. The ships they built to make good their boast were classic models of the North Atlantic's most colorful epoch.

Germany's Bid: The Imperial Family

With the coming of the twin-screw steamship and the consequent abandonment of auxiliary sails, the ocean liners of the late nineteenth century had lost their remaining family resemblance to the windjammers.[1] The Atlantic greyhounds of the 1890's had the basic appearance of today's ships. Passenger accomodations had moved out of the ship's hull into a superstructure above decks. The smooth, unbroken hull lines of the early steam packets were a thing of the past, but the big steamships of the 90's had only two or three decks above the hull. This gave them a somewhat lower, racier appearance than that of today's big ships with their towering, hotel-like superstructures. It also made them safer and better sea boats.

With their lean, slim hulls, low superstructures, and tall, raked funnels, these ships *looked* like ocean greyhounds, and it was in their era that the term was first used. It was at this period . . . the close of the nineteenth century . . . that the two great German lines, North German Lloyd and Hamburg-American, made their bid for supremacy on the Atlantic. The result was a quartette of marvelously swift and beautiful ships; the crowning shipbuilding achievement of the century.

The first of these was the *Kaiser Wilhelm Der Grosse*, and she set the pattern for the others. Built by Vulcan, at Stettin, she was 627 feet long with a

[1] The French Line's *La Touraine* of 1891 was the last Atlantic liner equipped with sails.

GERMAN GREYHOUND OF THE SEA: Kaiser Wilhelm II.

tonnage of 14,349. Two gigantic triple-expansion engines drove twin screws, giving her a speed of better than 22 knots. Of course she paid the usual price of high speed; her battery of furnaces devoured a ton of coal an hour for each knot of speed. Her array of furances vented in four massive funnels, spaced in pairs and gracefully raked. With the black coal smoke streaking aft from her four tall stacks, the white foam snoring at her trembling bow, she was a lovely sight as she slashed her way along the North Atlantic road. Launched early in 1897, she had broken all existing speed records before the year was out. She held the Blue Riband for North German Lloyd for the next three years, until the Hamburg-American Line brought out their *Deutschland*. A little bigger than the *Kaiser*, she was built to much the same plan, and most people thought the two were sister ships. Developing a speed of better than 24 knots, the *Deutschland* held the mythical speed trophy for a short time. Then the North Ger-

man Lloyd began building new ships, all similar in appearance to the beautiful *Kaiser Wilhelm Der Grosse*, but each one, as it appeared, developing somewhat higher speed. The *Kronprinz Wilhelm* was the first of these, taking the record back from the Hamburg-American Line. The *Kronprinz* was followed by the *Kaiser Wilhelm II and Kronprinzessin Cecilie*.

These great German liners made such names for themselves that they set a new pattern in the outward appearance of ocean liners for many years. Since they all had four funnels, the public came to look upon this as a sign of maritime distinction. When the British made a determined drive to regain their prestige in the early years of the twentieth century their greatest liners were all equipped with four stacks—whether they needed them or not. The *Mauretania, Lusitania, Aquitania, Olympic* and *Titanic* all followed this trend. Now the movement seems to be in the opposite direction. The *Aquitania* was the last

10

cruise ship before the First World War. In the process her speed was so reduced that she wasn't used in the war years and consequently lived to meet her fate at the hands of shipbreakers in 1925. The *Kaiser Wilhelm II* and *Kronprinzessin Cecilie* were caught in American ports at the outbreak of the First World War and were taken over as troopships. As the transport *Mount Vernon*, the old *Kronprinzessin Cecilie* was torpedoed by a German U-Boat off the French coast. The torpedo struck one of the engine rooms, which was immediately sealed off by the closure of the water-tight doors. The screams of the trapped and drowning engine room crew could be heard throughout the ship, but there was nothing that could be done for them. With the flooded compartment sealed off, the ship managed to reach Brest, where 36 bodies were taken from the flooded engine room; the ship repaired and put back into service. During the second big war she was broken up for scrap and used once more against her German builders.

The *Kronprinz Wilhelm* had the most thrilling career of all. With the outbreak of war in 1914 the lean greyhound of the sea became a stalking bloodhound. Armed as a raider, she prowled the seas for almost a year, sinking some 60,000 tons of British

of the four-stackers, and she went to the scrapper's yard in 1950. The giant *Queen Mary* is down to three, and the newer *Queen Elizabeth* has a mere two; no self-respecting emigrant who could count would have ridden on her in 1899!

Most of the big German greyhounds led exciting lives and some of them came to violent ends. The *Kaiser Wilhelm Der Grosse* barely escaped destruction in the great Hoboken pier fire of 1900, but she was towed to safety in the nick of time and lived to become an Imperial German naval cruiser. Off the coast of Africa in 1914, she was cornered by the British cruiser *Highflyer* and blown to pieces by gun fire.[2] The *Deutschland* had been converted into a

---

[2] Painted all black, the long, lean *Kaiser* looked extremely sinister, but she was actually not very effective as a cruiser. After sinking a trawler and the British steamer *Hyades* she cornered two British liners, but when her captain found they had women and children aboard he allowed them to proceed with a gallantry worthy of his gallant ship. When lack of coal (even at half speed she burned 250 tons a day) forced the German raider into the bay of Rio de Oro, the captain of H. M. S. *Highflyer*, with equal courtesy, accepted the surrender of the German crew before turning his guns on the *Kaiser Wilhelm der Grosse*.

HAPAG RACER DEUTSCHLAND won the Blue Riband of the Atlantic, but was not a consistent performer and ended up in lower speed cruise service.

—JOE WILLIAMSON PHOTO

shipping. The whole British Navy was alerted to intercept her, but it was not until her supplies and fuel were almost gone, her engines in need of repair, and most of her crew down with scurvy, that she decided to give up the fight. The United States wasn't in the war then . . . it was the Spring of 1915 . . . so it was agreed to run her into an American port for internment.

As she steamed up over the curve of the world, making for Hampton Roads, it was seen that the Chesapeake Bay entrance was being patrolled by half a dozen grim British warships. The cruisers were stationed at no more than half mile intervals, their guns covering every possible angle of approach. It looked completely hopeless for the sea-battered German raider.

But the *Kronprinz Wilhelm* was not a ship to give up easily. Night was falling; the darkness would give her a fighting chance. The last of the fuel was shoveled to the raging furnaces. Steaming at 16 knots when land was sighted, her speed increased steadily. The cranks and mighty eccentrics of her worn engines blurred with speed. On the bridge the indicators climbed to 20 knots—to 23 knots, the best speed she had ever made on her passenger runs when her engines were new and she was straining for the Blue Riband of the Atlantic. It seemed impossible,

but still the gauges climbed—to 24—to 25! The worn-out engines were breaking their hearts for the ship. They seemed to leap clear off the bed-plates in the frenzy of their insane speed. The boilers throbbed with the bursting force of a steam pressure their builders had never dreamed of. The whole great hull trembled until the German crewmen had to hold to rails and stanchions to keep from being shaken off their feet.

Out of the night she came, the sky glowing red above the crowns of her belching funnels, the white glow of acres of foam at her bow. The guns of the British cruisers swung around as the Aldis lamps blinked from the fighting tops.

But it was too late to bring those guns to bear. Between two startled British cruisers the German raider swept like an express train running on a track of foam . . . past them and into Hampton Roads without a scratch.

But the great ship had, in truth, broken her heart in that last, supreme effort. When America entered the war she was seized by the government, but it was found that the mighty engines and racing hull had been so strained and weakened that she would require major rebuilding when her war service was over. The work was never done, and she lay idly at dock until 1923, when she was sold for scrap.

RAKISH GERMAN FOUR-STACKER Kronprinz Wilhelm made dramatic dash through blockading British cruisers in World War I.

That ended the history of Germany's Imperial Family; the fleet of great four-stacked ocean liners that set the pace on the North Atlantic at the turn of the century. They were the greatest ships ever built by men who placed their faith in reciprocating engines for high speed. After them came the turbines.

The Greatest Ocean Liner of Them All: Mauretania

Since 1902 the Cunard Line had been laying plans to win back the Blue Riband of the Atlantic from the Germans. The first tentative plans called for a pair of big liners to be equipped with even more powerful reciprocating engines driving triple screws. After the early success of the Parsons turbine, however, some thought was given to equipping them with this new form of power in place of the old fashioned up-and-downers. But the Cunard hadn't lost its conservatism. There must be no mistakes. The new ships had to beat the Germans.

The Admiralty had not been stopped by the loss of the ill-fated turbine destroyers *Viper* and *Cobra*. New and faster destroyers and a cruiser had been built with turbines. The cross-channel packets were beginning to use them with fine results, and the Allen Line put their *Victorian* and *Virginian* into service with turbine engines. But the two Allen liners were in the Canadian service, where high speed wasn't required, and they were only 19-knot ships. Channel packets and navy ships weren't express liners looking for the world championship. Cunard had to be sure. They used the system they had used in 1862 when it was a question of paddle wheel or screw propeller. They built two sister ships, *Coronia* and *Carmania*. They were identical except for their

13

FIRST CUNARD TURBINE LINER, CARMANIA of 1904, paved the way for construction of the early twentieth century super-liners **Lusitania** and **Mauretania**.

engines. The *Caronia* was a twin screw ship with quadruple-expansion engines. *Carmania* had triple screws and turbines. The turbine liner was far less costly to operate and a bit faster than the up-and-downer. That settled it. The specifications of the two

Verandah Cafe of R.M.S. **Mauretania,** 1910

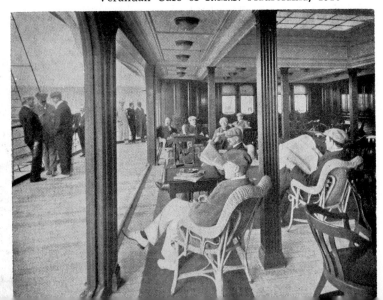

super-liners which were to bring the Blue Riband back to Britain called for Parsons turbines in the engine rooms.

The *Lusitania* and the *Mauretania* were ready for service late in 1907. They were very similar in appearance, but not quite sister ships. The *Lusitania* was 785 feet long over all, the *Mauritania* 790. They were four-funnel liners, with lines so graceful and lovely that they impressed people with their beauty more than their bulk, although they were the largest ships afloat. Turbines of 68,000 horsepower turned their quadruple screws. *Lusitania* was launched first and passed her trials at better than 25 knots. On her second crossing she won the Blue Riband from the Germans.

Then *Mauretania* took to the water and proceeded to ease through her trial runs at better than 26 knots. She remained a shade faster than her near sister, and she lived much longer. America moved close to the fighting when a German submarine torpedoed *Lusitania* off the Irish coast in 1915. The great ship was gone in 18 minutes; almost 1200 people died, and 124

FIRST OF THE TURBINE-DRIVEN super-liners, Cunard's splendid **Lusitania** fell victim to a German U-boat in 1915. Her sinking helped bring the United States into the conflict.
—JOE WILLIAMSON PHOTO

of them were Americans. But *Mauretania* lived on and grew greater with the years. She got oil burners and mechanical changes after serving as a World War I hospital ship. These increased her horsepower to 90,000 and her average speed to better than 27 knots. Once, during a sprint, the indicators reached 30 knots. From 1907 until 1929 that gallant and unconquerable ship held the Blue Riband of the Atlantic . . . twenty-two years of ceaseless racing back and forth across the storm-lashed North Atlantic, and she was never beaten! The lovely *Mauretania* was Queen of the North Atlantic for almost a quarter of all the time that steamships have raced for the mythical Blue Ribbon. A few great names stand out in the minds of men who know and love ships. There is something of beauty and romance in every ship, but a few ships seem to hold the very essence of that beauty and that romance. Such a ship was *Mauretania*. She stirred the imagination of men in all walks of life, from the grimy stokers in her holds to kings and presidents. Franklin D. Roosevelt, a man who knew and loved

ships, had a special place in his heart for *Mauretania*. What follows is his story of that great ship. It was written in 1936 . . . shortly after she left the United States on her last voyage . . . to the shipbreakers' yard. He entrusted the story to his friend, Ralph Cropley, with permission to release it for publication after his death. It appeared in the British magazine *Sea Breezes*, in 1950. It is reproduced here, in slightly abridged form, for the first time in the United States.

Deck games on R.M.S. **Lusitania,** 1910

R.M.S. TITANIC, FLAGSHIP OF THE WHITE STAR LINE, steamed majestically from Southampton on her maiden voyage in April, 1912. As the newspaper reproduction at the lower right shows, her collision with an ice berg off the Newfoundland Banks was not at first considered a major disaster. It was soon learned that hers was the most terrible tragedy in the history of ocean travel. For more than half a century the tragedy of the **Titanic** has been re-enacted in motion pictures. One of the earliest (1914) was advertised in the poster at the upper right. (Alert ship-identifiers may note that the picture labeled "S.S. Titanic leaving Southampton" is really one of the German four-stackers entering New York.

Queen with a Fighting Heart

By FRANKLIN D. ROOSEVELT

For 28 years the *Mauretania* played a poignant part not only in the maritime history of the world, but in business life, as well as being of inestimable service to the United States in time of war. When she was born in 1907 the *Mauretania* was the largest thing ever put together by man. For almost 22 years she remained the fastest liner he had ever produced. Even after she lost her world championship for size and speed she remained the world's most famous steamship. For it wasn't just her size or her speed that had given the *Mauretania* her fame. That rested on something more secure and intangible — on her personality, for the *Mauretania* was a ship with a fighting heart. If she hadn't been, Americans from all over the United States wouldn't pause before her 18-foot model in the Smithsonian Institution—pause, almost in reverence, and re-count, in awed voices, her history to their children.

Almost shaping history, the *Mauretania* made history as a carrier of human freight, bringing civilian men and women as well as American and Canadian soldiers to and fro across the Atlantic. And through the difficult years of history she lived in, the *Mauretania* never fell short of success. For she was a marked individuality, moving across 28 years of a period in which success was not easily attained.

On July 2, 1935, three extraordinary coincidences occurred—at least they were to me. On that date the 18-foot model of the *Mauretania*, which had been given to me by Bob Blake, American head of the Cunard Line, through Ralph Cropley, was installed in the "choosey" halls of the Smithsonian Institution. On that very date the real *Mauretania* herself bade goodbye to her birthplace at Newcastle-on-Tyne and sailed away to Scotland to be broken up. Also, on that very date, Ralph Cropley, who these 40 years has helped me with ship data, became 50 years old. Not that the last point is of any real importance, as Mr.

AT PANTAGES

Unequaled Vaudeville—Our Policy Never Changes.

All Week—Matinee Daily; Twice Nightly.

First Showing in the West of Klein's Sensational Mechanical Reproduction of

SINKING OF THE TITANIC

WORLD'S GREATEST SEA TRAGEDY

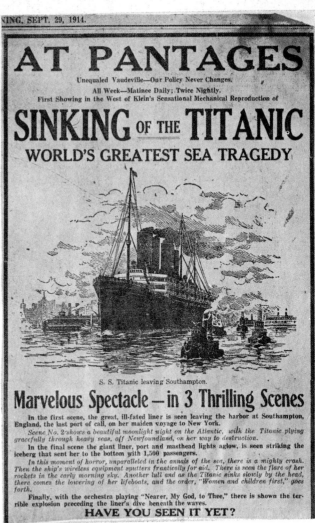

S. S. Titanic leaving Southampton.

Marvelous Spectacle — in 3 Thrilling Scenes

In the first scene, the great, ill-fated liner is seen leaving the harbor at Southampton, England, the last port of call, on her maiden voyage to New York.

Scene No. 2 shows a beautiful moonlight night on the Atlantic, with the Titanic plying gracefully through heavy seas, off Newfoundland, on her way to destruction.

In the final scene the giant liner, port and masthead lights aglow, is seen striking the iceberg that sent her to the bottom with 1,500 passengers.

In this moment of horror, unparalleled in the annals of the sea, there is a mighty crash. Then the ship's wireless equipment sputters frantically for aid. There is seen the flare of her rockets in the early morning sky. Another lull and as the Titanic sinks slowly by the head, there comes the lowering of her lifeboats, and the order, "Women and children first," goes forth.

Finally, with the orchestra playing "Nearer, My God, to Thee," there is shown the terrible explosion preceding the liner's dive beneath the waves.

HAVE YOU SEEN IT YET?

NEXT PAGES: R.M.S. AQUITANIA last of the four-funnel ocean liners.

Tacoma Daily Ledger.

HINGTON, MONDAY, APRIL 15, 1912.   MEMBER ASSOCIATED PRESS.   PRICE 5 CENTS.

Steamship Titanic on Her Maiden Voyage

TITANIC STRIKES ICEBERG; SINKING

Gigantic Vessel, With 1,300 Passengers on Board, Reports Disaster by Wireless and Aid Is Rushing Toward Her.

CANNOT REACH SCENE UNTIL 10 O'CLOCK TODAY

At Last Word From the Vessel, the Passengers Were Taking to the Boats and the Big Ship Was Going Down---Many Notable Americans on Board.

CAPE RACE, N. F., April 15—At 10:25 o'clock last night the steamship Titanic called C Q D and reported having struck an iceberg. The steamer said that immediate assistance was required.

Half an hour afterward another message came reporting that they were sinking by the head and that women were being put off in the life boats.

The weather was calm and clear, the Titanic's wireless operator reported, and the position of the vessel 46:46 north latitude and 50:54 west longitude.

The Marconi station at Cape Race notified the Allan liner Virgin

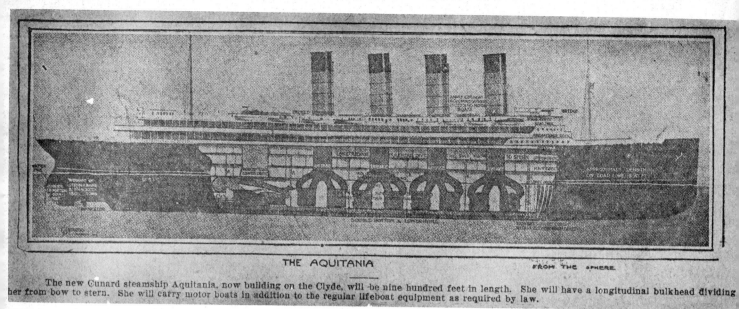

THE AQUITANIA

FROM THE SPHERE

The new Cunard steamship Aquitania, now building on the Clyde, will be nine hundred feet in length. She will have a longitudinal bulkhead dividing her from bow to stern. She will carry motor boats in addition to the regular lifeboat equipment as required by law.

NEWSPAPERS OF 1913 were filled with advance information on that forthcoming wonder of the maritime world, Cunard's huge AQUITANIA. The upper picture showed her interior plan.

Cropley himself would insist, other than a strange coincidence, for people are reaching 50 years every day. Yet somehow to me, parked as I am in the White House at Washington, there seems to be a weird connection between the three—something almost uncanny.

For years before I became President of the United States—while I was still Assistant Secretary of the Navy in the First World War—I wanted to see that the *Mauretania* should live in American history as she deserved, along with the *Clermont,* the *Savannah,* the *Flying Cloud,* the *Great Eastern,* the *Glory of the Seas,* which had made history as the *Mauretania* had. And let me assure you that the very "choosey" Smithsonian—the National Museum of the United States Government—did not accept her 18-foot model from me because it came to them as a gift of the President of the United States. In fact, the powers-that-be of the Smithsonian told me flatly that the institution accepted the model "because the *Mauretania* herself had *earned the right* to enter the hallowed halls of the United States Government's National Museum", along

with the Lindbergh and Wright planes and other history-making things. Yes, the President of the United States could have gone and cooled his heels if the *Mauretania* herself hadn't been a Queen with a fighting heart.

It must not be forgotten that of the many excellent liners of the first third of the 20th Century, and long before she was launched in the fall of 1906, the *Mauretania* had become the most discussed ship ever planned. Her design, her engines, and her luxuriousness have been so often and at such great length and detail set forth in print that any description of them by me would be out of place. She was 790 feet long, 88 feet beam, and 66½ feet molded depth, and her gross tonnage was 31,938.

Miss Marguerite Le Hand, my secretary, to whom I am dictating this yarn, advises me that when first commissioned the *Mauretania* could carry 2,165 passengers and a crew of 938. Her contract speed was 25 knots. Yet on many an Atlantic crossing she averaged 27 knots and more the whole way across (as she once did with me aboard). Why, even in her old age, this dowager had a burst of speed of 32 knots. In middle age she had her face lifted by being converted from a coal-burner to an oil-burner.

I well remember that the woodwork of her public rooms and corridors was unusually elaborate. Nothing like it will ever again be built into an Atlantic liner. The Latvian oak panels of her dining saloon, as I remember, were hand-carved, every one being "individually" different. But then the fame of the

Q.S.S. AQUITANIA.

PORT OF NEW YORK, North River Piers form legendary "Ocean Liner Row." At pierside on this late June day of 1960 were American Export Line's **Constitution,** Italian Lines' **Vulcania, America** of United States Lines, Transat's **Liberté,** and **Britannic, Queen Mary** and **Caronia** of Cunard-White Star. (Opposite page.)

—PORT OF NEW YORK AUTHORITY PHOTO

FOLLOWING PAGES: WHITE STAR LINER Olympic, sister-ship to the **Titanic,** arriving at New York.

21

FRANCO-AMERICAN FRIENDSHIP is graphically portrayed, opposite page, as Statue of Liberty, France's gift to the United States, stands watch over all-out welcome to S.S. **France,** majestic new flagship of Compagnie Generale Transatlantique and the world's longest ocean liner. Photograph taken at noon, February 8, 1962.

——PORT OF NEW YORK AUTHORITY PHOTO

Mauretania does not lie in the clothes she wore, but in what she stood for and the work she did. As the Smithsonian Institution said, in accepting the model from me, "It can truthfully be said that the *Mauretania* was the greatest advancement made in ship-building in generations."

Actually, her fame and the veneration in which the world holds her memory rest on the fact that during her 28 years of service she turned in a record of consistent performances, whether as a passenger liner, a hospital ship, or an American troop transport.

Every ship has a soul, but the *Mauretania* had one you could talk to . . . as Captain Rostron once said to me, she had the manners and deportment of a great lady, and behaved herself as such.

From notes "Missy" Le Hand has given me, I see that one year, for three consecutive voyages the *Mauretania* arrived at Cherbourg from New York with but a minute's difference in time for crossing the Atlantic. The times were 5:29 a.m., 5:30 a.m., and

MAURETANIA, ALWAYS A LOVELY SHIP, looked particularly handsome when painted white for special cruise service.

5:31 a.m. on Monday mornings after having left her New York dock the previous Wednesdays. Yes, she was a well-bred warrior with a fighting heart. She seems to have borne a charmed life. I note that in the World War she was only attacked once, though other ships about her were being torpedoed. She was never responsible for the death of a single person on her. She might flop seas on board which tore away deck railing and spattered the captain's dress shirt on the bridge, but that was but play. She was never vicious.

The *Mauretania* always fascinated me with her graceful, yachtlike lines, her four enormous black-topped red funnels, and her appearance of power and good breeding; especially was this so in the later years of her life when she was painted white for cruising and became known as the "White Queen" or, as some of her crew have said, "Looked like a bloomin' wedding cake."

Think of it! She held the Blue Ribbon of the Atlantic for 22 years and at that age went out and beat her own record. In 1929 she made an Atlantic crossing at 27.22 knots (if "Missy" Le Hand's notes are correct), beating her own record for the fastest crossing by four hours, only to be beaten by four and one-half hours by

the brand-new *Bremen*. To do New York City credit, while I was still Governor of New York State the city's waterfront gave her a wonderful reception in spite of the fact that Wall Street had gone crazy over the stock market slump. Yes, no matter what, we Americans are ever stirred by a decent sentiment. Her failure to beat a new ship especially designed at great expense to beat her fixed peoples' affection on her as much as her success ever had done.

I am going to quote from a letter I received from Ralph Cropley, who had done so much for the marine reference library of the Smithsonian Institution:

It was 5 p.m., Franklin, last Wednesday (September 26, 1934) that the stately and noble *Mauretania* bade goodbye to New York harbor, which knew and loved her for so many years. Slowly, silently, and majestically, the "White Queen" passed down the harbor as the commuters were going home on the ferries. An escort of courtesy she might have had for the asking on this, her farewell departure. But all her life the *Mauretania* had been going it alone.

Honestly, Franklin, it seemed as if the tide was desiring to assert a prerogative of conveying her to the open sea. Even the waves of the harbor seemed gently to kiss the sides of her as she gracefully glided

Granted the *Mauretania* had outlived her usefulness. Granted she had become economically unprofitable, killed by the public craze for needless swimming pools and private baths, which passengers rarely used the whole trip (other than the toilet) after they'd payed heavily for the foolish honor. But why couldn't the British have remembered the *Mauretania's* faithfulness—taken her out to sea and sunk her whole—giving her a Viking's funeral, this ship with a fighting heart? It would be more inspiring to those who come hereafter to know that a ship that was a ship received decent treatment at her death.

I am not recording my affection for the *Mauretania* as President of the United States, but as civilian Franklin D. Roosevelt, who loves the sea, its ships, and the men who sail them. It is meant solely as an historical record and a tale of my sea love.

CUNARD LINE COMMODORE HARRY GRATTIDGE, right, retired in December, 1953 after completing his final voyage on **Queen Elizabeth.** Following World War I naval service, he re-entered Cunard service as third officer of the old **Mauretania.** His book, **Captain of the Queens,** E. P. Dutton, 1956, is a fine tale of ocean liner life.

—CUNARD LINE PHOTO

through the water. Everything in the harbor seemed to have rested a while to look upon the scene of a grand old lady of the seas—the one "White Queen"—going to her doom, head up, regally.

Yes, from office windows in the skyscrapers, from the decks of the commuters' ferry boats (as I was on) many an eye beheld the cortege. And Americans that we are and British though she was, multitudes of hearts trembled with honest emotion at the passing of a grand old friend—an honored servant of both England and the United States in peace and war."

Mr. Cropley went on to say that others, besides himself, who had witnessed the "goodbye," kind of found it hard to work for several days after that. For to some of us, myself included, the sea persists in remaining romance, vaguely enticing, dimly alluring, always maintaining its distance. I'm sure that thousands of others besides myself and Ralph Cropley found it hard on July 2, 1935, when we read that the *Mauretania* was on her last voyage to the shipbreakers to be turned into shot and shell for the next war. It seemed almost blasphemous that a queen should have for her Valhalla only a newspaper paragraph.

HOLLAND-AMERICAN LINE'S fourth **Rotterdam** came out the same year as **George Washington** 1908, and was of similar dimensions . . . 24,149 tons, with a length of 650.5 feet. She ran successfully in Atlantic passenger service for 32 years. She was a twin-screw steamer powered by 8-cylinder quadruple-expansion engines.

—HOLLAND-AMERICA LINE PHOTO

The Unsinkable Ocean Liner: Titanic

After the arrival of the *Mauretania* and *Lusitania* in 1907 the trans-Atlantic lines gave up trying to build faster liners than the Cunard flyers. They concentrated on larger ships, which were a few knots slower than the champions on an average crossing, but could compete in luxury and gadgets. The advertising experts began to sell the public on the idea of the floating hotel, convincing the Atlantic traveler that he might just as well paddle across in a hollow log as to go in a ship that didn't have a tiled swimming pool, Turkish baths, gymnasium, and a dining saloon at least four stories high with a glass dome on top.

Such ships were the White Star Liners *Titanic* and *Olympic*, which were ready for service in 1911. They were the biggest ships afloat; 882 feet long, with a registered tonnage of 46,000 and a displacement tonnage of 66,000. The great hulls, four city blocks long, were divided by 15 water-tight bulkheads, but they were famed for their luxurious appointments rather than for the safety of their structure; it was taken for granted that such mighty ships were quite unsinkable. They had 11 decks; from the keel to the tops of their four mighty funnels they towered 175 feet; they had gymnasiums, swimming pools, hospitals, grills, palm gardens and royal suites. The *Great Eastern* of 1860 had none of these luxuries, but she had a double hull. The *Titanic* and *Olympic* didn't.

The two ships had an unusual, but practical and economical power system. They were triple screw ships, the two outboard propellers being driven by regular reciprocating steam engines. After the steam had been used to push the multiple cylinders of the two outboard engines, it was exhausted into a Parsons turbine amidships, which used the steam that would otherwise have been wasted in the condensers, to turn the center shaft. They steamed with little vibration at an average rate of 21 knots, and while they hadn't been built with the idea of challenging the *Mauretania* in speed, there were those who felt that by pushing them a bit, they might squeeze out a record passage or two under favorable conditions.

Ill fortune seemed to dog both ships from the start. The *Olympic* was rammed by the British cruiser

UNITED STATES LINER George Washington carried thousands of troops during second World War, was familiarly known as "Big George. She was originally a North German Lloyd Liner under the same name.

Hawke while on her maiden voyage. Her massive hull was torn open, but the water-tight bulkheads held and she was gotten into port for repairs. She managed to escape the torpedos of World War I, when she served as a trooper, but in 1934 she rammed and sank the *Nantucket* lightship off the New England coast, all hands aboard the lightship being lost. She went to the shipbreakers in 1935, as did the *Mauretania*.

The *Titanic* was destined for a shorter and far more tragic career. She made only one voyage.

It was a gala day at the White Star Piers in Southampton on Wednesday, April 10, 1912, for the mighty *Titanic* was ready for her first trans-Atlantic voyage. The great bellow of her sirens drowned out the rollicking tune the band was playing on her boat deck and the excited cheers of the crowds on shore; then the lines came in and the ship's massive bulk moved in slow majesty from the land. The towering bow turned toward the sea. Then the imps of bad luck took over. The *Titanic* displaced 66,000 tons of water. Marine architects hadn't quite mastered the art of designing hulls of such monstrous proportions able to slip smoothly through the water. As she passed down the stream the immense moving bulk of the *Titanic* drew the water after her with the power of a maelstrom. The irresistable suction tore the old American liner *New York* from her moorings, snapping her steel mooring lines like rotten string. The smaller liner was drawn toward the *Titanic* as if by invisible magnets, and it looked as if a collision was inevitable. In the nick of time the big tugs *Neptune* and *Vulcan* foamed out to get lines aboard the *New York,* dig in their heels, and hold her while the *Titanic* continued her stately passage toward the sea.

The passengers witnessed this exciting near-disaster, but they didn't know that fire was raging in the *Titanic's* bunkers almost from the time she left the dock. Spontaneous combustion had set the fuel supply on fire, and two men from each watch of stokers did nothing but fight the blaze until the voyage ended in a debacle that blotted out all such minor hazards.

After putting in at Cherbourg and Queenstown, the *Titanic* began her final dash for America. The first day out her mighty engines loafed along at 70 revolutions a minute. Her day's run was 484 miles. The

THE GIANT GERMAN twins **Europa** and **Bremen** ended the 22-year reign of **Mauretania** as speed queen of the North Atlantic. **Bremen** was destroyed by allied bombing in World War II, but **Europa** lived to begin a new career in 1950 as the French Line's **Liberte**, remaining in service until 1962.

—JOE WILLIAMSON PHOTO

second day the beat of the screws rose to 73 revolutions; the day's run was posted at 519 miles. The third day, Sunday, the engines speeded up to 75, which gave the liner her contract speed of 21 knots and a day's run of 549 miles. There was no doubt that another three revolutions could be safely turned, and Captain E. J. Smith, master of the *Titanic* and commodore of the White Star fleet, announced that if Monday were fair he'd ring her up to 78 turns a minute and show the passengers what the great ship could really do in the way of speed. The passengers looked forward to the exciting prospect, but for the *Titanic,* and for most of them, Monday never came.

The liner was racing the northern trans-Atlantic lane, the shortest one, and by Sunday evening she was fast approaching the Grand Banks of Newfoundland. Wireless had gone to sea with the liners of the 20th Century, and on Sunday afternoon the *Titanic's* Marconi operator forwarded this message to the weather stations in the Atlantic seaboard of America:

April 14.—German S.S. Amerika, Hamburg-American Line, reports by radio-telegraph passing two large icebergs in latitude 41.27, longitude 50.08.,—Titanic, Br. S.S.

But the *Titanic* paid no heed to her own warning. Sunday night found her forging on toward the Grand Banks with no reduction in speed. The sea was placid and the sky bright with stars, although there was no moon visible. Sometimes the great bow wave flung a drifting scum of ice from the liner's path. Small, harmless-looking ice-floes were set to rocking by the widening V of the rushing steamship's wake. After 11 o'clock the lookouts in the crowsnest phoned warnings to the watch officer on the bridge. They thought they could see the glimmer of icebergs in the distant darkness. But there was no signal for reduced speed to engineers below. On the *Titanic* rushed at a speed of 21 to 23 knots.

At 11:37 the bridge telephone rang again. It wasn't answered until a fatal lapse of two minutes or so. It was the lookout again. This time there was no question about it. A gigantic ice mountain lay square in the speeding liner's path. If the warning had been heeded two minutes earlier there might have been time to swerve the ship in her headlong rush, avoiding the berg entirely or, at the worst, grazing it with her stern. If there had been no warning at all she would have rammed it head-on and might have lived to

A LONG AND COSTLY reconstruction program resulted in the former **Europa's** debut with an entirely new personality as the elegant French **Liberte.**

sail again. As it was, the factors of time and distance coincided to bring about the worst possible disaster.

As the chief officer turned from the telephone to the wheel house he had one terrifying glimpse of a massive blue bulk of ice looming ahead. His orders were instinctive:

Hard Astarboard! For God sake put the helm over hard!

In the darkened wheel house of the *Titanic* the quartermaster swung the wheel to full left rudder. Then the mate sprang to the engine room telegraphs. Far below the bells jangled wildly. Alert engineers leaped to the controls. The starboard engine raced on full ahead. The port engine swung to a stop with a sudden gentle sigh of escaping steam. Then the great mass of moving steel flashed into action again . . . *Full speed astern on the port engine!*

With helm hard down, with one wing engine racing full ahead, the other full astern, the 66,000-ton *Titanic* spun on her heel, dodging for her life. It was that sudden effort to escape that was the death of her. Instead of striking the iceberg head on the ship's whole starboard side dragged along the frozen mountain. The knife-like edge of submerged ice pierced the hull well forward, the speed and bulk of the ship did the rest. The hidden fangs cut through nearly the

whole length of the ship's underbody as she swept on, knifing through the steel plates the way a sharp can-opener lays open a tomato tin.

Cushioned by the thousands of tons of hull structure, the shock wasn't great and the passengers were not alarmed. Some already in bed and asleep, weren't even awakened. Card players in the smoking room looked up briefly; then went on with their games. When Captain Smith reached the bridge he ordered the water-tight doors closed. That had already been done, but the *Titanic* was already listing five degrees to starboard and settling down fast at the bow. Distress rockets went soaring from the bridge into the star-flecked sky. From the Marconi-wires the disaster call crackled in blue sparks . . . *C.Q.D. — S.O.S. — We have struck an iceberg. We are badly damaged. Send help!*

The wireless station at Cape Race picked up the call and so did a score of ships at sea. From 170 miles away the *Virginian* heard the *Titanic* calling for help. Smoke pouring from her stack, she turned in her tracks and raced for the disaster scene. Nearby the Cunarder *Carpathia*, outward bound for the Mediterranean, heard the call too, and she raced back toward the *Titanic* under forced draft. The big White Star liner *Baltic*, 200 miles to the southeast, heard and

GRACE AND POWER were combined in the Italian Line's 880-foot **Rex**, above, built by the Ansaldo yard at Genoa. In 1933 she won the Blue Riband from **Europa**, the only ship sailing from a Mediterranean port ever to be recognized as speed queen of the Atlantic.

—ITALIAN LINE PHOTO

BELOW: PROMENADE DECK, Writing Room, **Queen Mary.**

responded. All along the northern sea-lane the Atlantic liners changed course and crowded on steam as the *Titanic's* death call reached them. Far to the eastward her mighty sister, *Olympic*, made a great white half-circle in the dark water and foamed westward again. The German four-stackers heard the call, and so did many other ships. They all turned toward the circle of black, ice-dotted sea where the *Titanic* lay sinking.

While the rockets soared and the Marconi set stuttered over its jumping blue spark, the steam-sirens at the towering stack-brims took up their soul-shattering cry for help. Through all that transpired after that, until the mighty liner took her final plunge, the sirens sobbed their eerie obligato to the tragedy that went on below them.

When it finally dawned upon both passengers and crew that *Titanic* . . . the mighty, the unsinkable *Titanic* . . . *was* sinking, and sinking fast, preparations were made to abandon ship. Then the passengers discovered an interesting fact; something that no one had thought of when they were busy admiring the tiled swimming pool, the tennis courts, the palm room, and the electric elevators. *There were not enough lifeboats to hold everyone on the* Titanic!

The ship carried 20 lifeboats and liferafts. Filled to their utmost capacity they would have carried 1,100 persons. There were 2,340 aboard the *Titanic.* No

ABOVE: WHEEL HOUSE of Queen Mary, with quartermaster at the helm; radar equipment in center foreground. Below: Ballroom and First Class Lounge, **Queen Elizabeth.**
—CUNARD LINE PHOTO

FOLLOWING PAGES: ONE OF THE greatest ocean liners of all time, the magnificent French Liner **Normandie** had a short but brilliant career; was destroyed by fire at her New York pier after being taken over by the U. S. government as the transport **Lafayette.**

crews had been assigned to the boats; no boat drills had been held. Four of the boats were wrecked in launching. The boats that survived could have carried 928 people. They actually took off just over 700.

At 17 minutes past midnight the onrushing rescue ships heard the last signal from *Titanic's* wireless. Lower and lower she sank in the still water, her great bow dipping close to the surface, the stern, with its three great propellers exposed, rising into the night sky. The ship's officers drew revolvers to enforce the unwritten sea code, *women and children first.* One by one the boats dropped into the water and rowed away. They were almost entirely filled with women and children, but there were exceptions. Bruce Ismay, managing director of the White Star Line, was in one of the first boats away from the sinking liner. Legend has it that two gamblers, dressed in women's clothing, reached safety in the boats. Not all the women would leave in the boats. Some preferred the broad deck of the liner to the dark unknown of a tiny lifeboat in an icy sea. Some would not leave their husbands, and the men must stay with the ship. Old Mrs. Isidor Straus, wife of the multi-millionaire founder of Macy's Department Store, was one who elected to stay. "We are too old to leave each other," she said, "we can best die together."

From the boats the death of the *Titanic* was an awesome spectacle. The bows sanks until the water was level with the captain's bridge. An hour before it had been 90 feet above the water. The massive stern rose higher as the bow sank, but the eleven rows of lights that marked the liner's decks glowed brightly still. Between the shattering blasts of the sirens the orchestra could be heard playing on the boat deck, as they had done at Southampton on the gala sailing day. *Nearer My God to Thee* they were playing now, and many of those left to die aboard the *Titanic* took up the words of the majestic hymn. The sound drifted across the quiet water to the people in the boats and then was silenced by the hoarse sobbing of the sirens.

Finally the stern rose almost straight into the air. There was an awful rumble—an earthquake sound. It was the ponderous machinery of the *Titanic*, torn loose and hurtling downward, crashing through the bulkheads to the sunken bow. The lights went out then, and the great sirens cried no more. But faintly, across the dark waters, the strains of the orchestra still came. It was the lovely old hymn *Autumn*. . . .

> *Hold me up in mighty waters,*
> *Keep my eyes on things above—*

After that there was only silence, broken by the faint, distant crying of hundreds of the *Titanic's* people dying in the icy North Atlantic water. In less than an hour and a half from the sighting of the iceberg the world's greatest steamship was gone, slowly drifting down through 16,000 feet of water to the ocean's floor.

Before dawn *Carpathia* came through the floating ice to pick up the *Titanic's* boats. A few more than 700 of the company of more than 2,300 that had left Southampton so gayly lived to reach the decks of the *Carpathia*. The rest died with the ship that couldn't sink.

The world was stunned when the full tidings of the disaster were released. It was known that the *Titanic* had struck an iceberg, but everyone aboard was thought to have been saved. The true facts were slow in resolving themselves from the welter of rumors and counter-rumors, but when they had at last been made starkly clear, there was a tremendous public outcry. American ships had long been required to carry enough lifeboats to accommodate all on board, but foreign ships had been allowed to carry passengers from American ports without such precautions. Now Americans wanted to know why.

Congress knew why. The foreign lines were cleaning up in the emigrant trade, carrying hordes of European refugees like cattle in their steerage quarters. There were no alien quotas then, and it was a golden harvest. The steamships couldn't carry enough boats to take care of everyone when their holds were crammed with steerage passengers and their upper decks were littered with squash-courts and palm-bordered swimming pools for the elite. They had a lobby in the American Congress, the foreign steamship operators, and it had been an effective one. American safety regulations didn't protect Americans sailing on foreign ships.

So, like all great disasters, the sinking of the *Titanic* had some good results. The maritime laws of many European nations were overhauled. Foreign ships were required to meet American safety standards if they wanted to carry passengers from American ports. Ship builders incorporated that old reliable device, the double bottom, in future vessels. But most important of all, a state of mind was corrected. Even the *Titanic's* master, who paid with his life for his error, was sure his ship was unsinkable. Her loss brought home the great and simple truth that there has never been and never will be an unsinkable ship. That only eternal vigilance by men can win the eternal battle with the sea.

New Queens of the North Atlantic

Although the phenomenal performance of the *Mauretania* discouraged attempts to take the Blue Riband from her for more than two decades, great ships were built by the maritime nations of the Atlantic . . . British express liners, French *paquebots* and German *schnelldampfer*. Larger and more luxurious ships than the gallant *Mauretania* were launched even before the first World War. Notable among these were the giant *Olympic* and her ill-fated sister, *Titanic* of the White Star Line, Cunard's beautiful four-stacker *Aquitania*, the luxurious French Line four-stacker *France* and the huge *Imperator*, *Vaterland* and *Bismarck* of the German Hamburg-American Line.

After the first World War the three German sea giants were turned over to British and American owners, the *Imperator* becoming the Cunarder *Berengaria*, the *Vaterland* the United States Line's *Leviathan*, and the *Bismark* the White Star liner *Majestic*.

These ships, and other first-class express liners of the period, were capable of high speed, but none of them enjoyed the power-to-weight ratio required to beat the mighty *Mauretania*. It was not until 1929 that a liner was launched with the ability to take the Riband from the aging Cunarder; again it was the Germans who produced a ship, or rather a pair of ships, designed frankly to take the speed trophy from the British Merchant Navy.

The keel of the North German Lloyd's new liner *Bremen* was laid at the Weser Shipbuilding yards in Bremen on June 18, 1927. The keel of her sister ship, *Europa*, was laid at the Hamburg yards of Blohm & Voss on July 23 of the same year. The Germans had

CUNARD-ANCHOR CRUISE

CUNARD LINE

Twin-Screw

S. S. "CARONIA"

TONNAGE 20,000

OCTOBER 22nd and DECEMBER 7th 1921

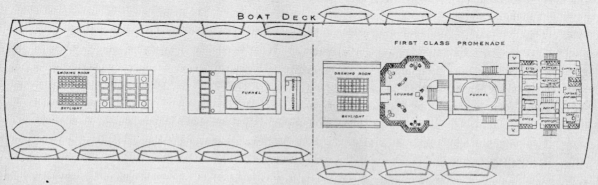

BOAT DECK

FIRST CLASS PROMENADE

DECK A (UPPER PROMENADE DECK)

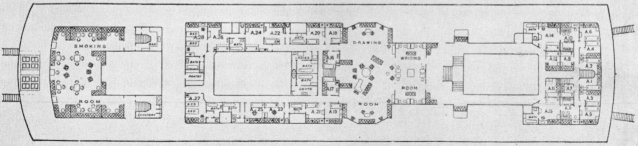

DECK B (PROMENADE DECK)

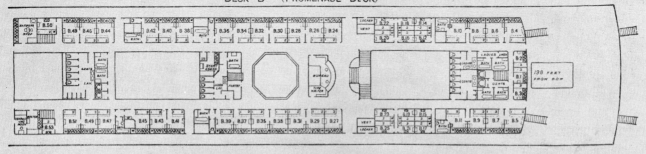

DECK C (SALOON DECK)

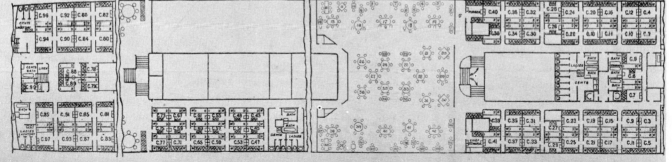

DECK D (UPPER DECK)

QUEEN ELIZABETH, current running-mate of Queen Mary in Cunard's primary trans-Atlantic service, was nosed out of her spot as world's longest liner by the new French Liner France in 1962; is still rated the largest. Preceding pages; Queen Mary.

—CUNARD LINE PHOTO

planned a dramatic dual launching, with the two ships to make their maiden voyages simultaneously. Both were launched in August, 1928, but a disastrous fire aboard the *Europa* delayed her completion by almost a year. The *Bremen*, finished on schedule, made her initial voyage in June, 1929, slashing her way across the North Atlantic from Cherbourg to Ambrose Light-ship in four days, 17 hours, 42 minutes, for an average speed of 27.83 knots. The *Bremen* had bettered the *Mauretania's* best average crossing speed by a scant fifty-eight hundredths of a knot, but it was sufficient to return the Blue Riband to Germany.

When the *Europa* made her delayed debut she took the trophy away from her sister, making the crossing in four days, 17 hours, six minutes, an average speed of 27.91 knots. For a time both *Bremen* and *Europa* carried a plane which was catapulted from the deck when the ship was a day's steaming from port, thus delivering the trans-Atlantic mails a day earlier than even their racing schedule would have permitted.

The *Bremen* and *Europa* were the first of the modern express liners designed to be fast enough to cross the Atlantic, refuel, load passengers and stores and be ready for the return voyage within a single week. This schedule permitted the two liners to maintain a weekly trans-Atlantic express service, a schedule which until then had always required the services of three or four ships. Their speed thus had practical applications beyond those of prestige and national pride.

Like the earlier German four-stackers of World War I days, the *Bremen* and *Europa* had their share of adventure during the second World War. *Bremen* was at dock in New York when war broke out in 1939. She fled at once for Germany with all the thrust of her 130,000-horsepower quadruple screws. Although Allied air and surface fleets combed the Atlantic, intent upon her capture, she seemed to have vanished like a maritime ghost. Steaming far north of the regular shipping lanes, she had crossed by way of Green-

CUNARD'S SECOND MAURETANIA, completed in 1939 is, at 35,674 tons, a bigger ship than her famous namesake, the first **Mauretania,** but is considered a medium-sized liner by present-day standards.

—CUNARD LINE PHOTO

land, then north of Iceland to the northern coast of Norway. Then she hugged the Norwegian coast until she reached German waters and the safety of her home port.

Her respite was brief, however, for during the allied bombings of the Port of Bremen she was hit and set on fire. So badly was she damaged that the Germans were forced to make scrap of their maritime pride, her remains going to the munitions factories of the Ruhr.

Europa, having already survived a major fire that almost ended her career before it began, had better luck. She stayed safely afloat in her home port throughout the war, although there were many rumors that she was on the high seas serving as an armed cruiser. Upon the occupation of Germany, *Europa* was taken over by the United States Navy for a brief period as a trooper, returning American soldiers from Europe. After two voyages in this service, the Inter-Allied Reparations Commission awarded her to France

in May, 1946. In June of that year she was rechristened *Liberte* and moved to the Penhoet Shipyards at St. Nazaire, arriving there in November, 1947, for the long and costly job of refitting.

While *Liberte* lay at the refitting dock, a tremendous gale struck the French coast, tearing the giant liner from her moorings and driving her against the sunken hull of the French liner *Paris.* A gaping hole torn in her side, *Liberte* sank to the bottom of St. Nazaire harbor which is not, fortunately, very deep.

By the time she was raised and refitting completed, three years and almost twenty million dollars later, she was virtually a new ship. She was accorded the traditional honors accorded a new sea queen when she swept into New York harbor on her maiden voyage under French colors on August 17, 1950. Although she never competed again for the Blue Riband of the Atlantic, her reputation for luxury and superb French cuisine made her one of the most popular of the first-

VETERAN OF THE NORTH ATLANTIC, built in 1905 by Alexander Stephan & Sons, Glasgow as the **Virginian**, this ship with her sister-liner **Victorian**, inaugurated turbine propulsion for Atlantic liners. They were designed for Allan Line service between Liverpool and Canada and held the speed record until 1907 when the rival Canadian Pacific brought out the first **Empress of Britain** and **Empress of Ireland**. In 1920 **Virginian** was taken over by the Swedish-American Line as **Drottningholm**, in which service she's pictured above. Re-engined with geared turbines and converted to oil fuel in 1922, she served Sweden well until 1947, when she was sold to Panamanian Lines (later Home Lines) and renamed **Brasil**, entering the emigrant service between Italy and South America. In 1951, at the age of 46, this famous old ship was once more renamed, **Homeland**, for Greek Flag New York-Southampton service; was finally broken up at Trieste in 1955.

—SWEDISH-AMERICAN LINE PHOTO

HOLLAND'S GREATEST SHIP, and at 38,645 tons the largest liner ever built in the Netherlands, Holland-America Line's new flagship **Rotterdam** is 748 feet long with a beam of 94 feet; can carry 1,456 passengers in trans-Atlantic service and about half that many on cruises. She is the fifth **Rotterdam** to wear the green-white-green houseflag of the 89-year-old Dutch line. When she made her triumphal maiden entry to New York harbor on September 11, 1959 she passed the spot off Staten Island where exactly 350 years earlier to the day Henry Hudson had anchored his little carvel **Halve Maen** upon his discovery of "Nieuw Amsterdam."

—HOLLAND-AMERICAN LINE PHOTO

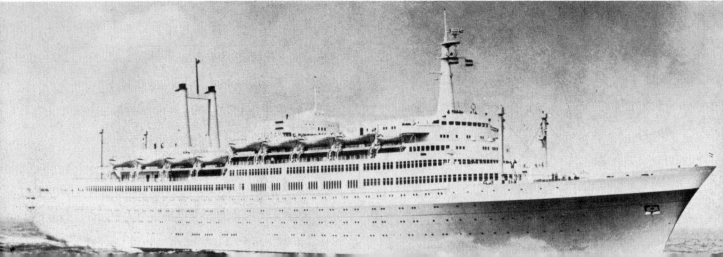

S.S. ISRAEL, BUILT FOR Zim Israel Navigation Company in 1955 by Deutscher Werft, Hamburg, and her sister-ship **Zion** sail every third week from New York to Haifa with calls at Medeira, Gibralter and Piraeus. Westbound they call at Cyprus, Naples, Marseilles, Gibralter and occasionally at Halifax. **Israel** is pictured above against the night-time backdrop of her home port, Haifa.

QUEEN WHO NEVER REIGNED, white Star Line's second **Britannic,** right, was launched in February, 1914, and completed after the outbreak of World War I. Incorporating all the hard-learned safety lessons resulting from the loss of **Titanic,** she was designed for the Southampton-Cherbourg-New York express run. Although employed as a hospital ship, she was sunk by mines laid by a German submarine in the Agean Sea late in 1916 and never made a commercial voyage. The first **Britannic,** lower left, led a longer and luckier life. Built by Harland & Wolff of Belfast (who also built the White Star **Britannics** of 1914 and 1930), she was considered a giant at 5,004 tons and 445 feet when she was launched in 1874. She was the first ship in the world, except for the **Great Eastern,** to exceed 5,000 tons. This famous liner won the Blue Riband in 1876; remained in service into the twentieth century, and was finally scrapped in 1903.

FOLLOWING PAGES: FRENCH SUPER-LINER France, at 1,035 feet in length, exceeds that of **Normandie** and **Queen Elizabeth,** previously the two longest liners ever built. **France** made her glamorous debut in 1962. She's now rated the longest, **Queen Elizabeth** the largest (tonnage-wise); **United States** the fastest.

WHITE STAR LINE'S GREAT STEAMSHIP BRITANNIC SUCCESSFULLY LAUNCHED AT YARDS OF BELFAST

Steamship Britannic as she will appear when completed.

QUEEN FREDERICA, formerly Matson Lines' **Malolo,** made her debut under the Home Lines' house-flag as the **Atlantic** in May, 1949. In 1954 the subsidiary National Hellenic American Line was formed and the 21,570-ton liner was assigned to operate between New York and Piraeus, via the Mediterranean, under her new name and the Greek flag.

class trans-Atlantic liners for the next twelve years. On November 10, 1952, she sailed from New York on her final voyage, soon to be replaced by the French Line's giant new *France.*

It was announced at the time that *Liberte* had been purchased for use during the summer of 1962 as a floating hotel and entertainment center at Seattle World's Fair, but the deal fell through and, as this is written, the great old Atlantic racer is being demolished at the scrapyards at La Spezia, Italy.

The *Bremen* and *Europa* had already surrendered the Blue Riband well before the outbreak of the war. It went to the handsome new Italian Liner *Rex* in August of 1933, when she steamed east from Gibralter to Ambrose Lightship . . . 3,181 miles . . . in four days, 13 hours, 58 minutes, for an average speed of 28.92 knots. Like her German contemporaries, she was laid up when war broke out, but on September 9, 1944, while being towed to a new hideout, she was attacked and sunk by British torpedo planes. By that time, she too had lost the speed trophy.

The new winner was the gigantic super-liner *Normandie,* first to win the title for the French since the brief reign of *La Touraine* in 1891. Combining grace and beauty with her tremendous size (with a length of 1,027 feet she still rates as the third longest liner ever built, exceeded only by the *Queen Elizabeth,* 1,031 feet, and the new *France,* 1,035 feet), the *Normandie* was built for the Compagnie Generale Transatlantique (French Line) by Penhoet at St. Nazaire. Driven by turbines generating 160,000-horsepower, the *Normandie* won the Blue Riband from the *Rex* on her first voyage by making the westward crossing at an average speed of 29.94 knots, a performance which she promptly bettered by returning at 30.31 knots.

Normandie reigned unchallenged on the North Atlantic until the late summer of 1936 when Cunard placed the gallant *Queen Mary* in service. The hull of the 1,020-foot *Queen* had been laid at the Clydebank yards of John Brown and Company shortly after the advent of *Bremen* and *Europa,* but construction was suspended for two years due to financial problems and she was not completed until 1936. After that she and *Normandie* fought it out for top honors until the war ended their rivalry, and the life of the great French liner.

The *Queen Mary's* maiden voyage in May, 1936 was not as spectacular as that of *Normandie.* It was

a foggy crossing and no records were broken; but in August of that year the full thrust of her 200,000-horsepower turbines was unleashed and she claimed the westward crossing record at an average speed of 30.01 knots. On the return voyage she claimed the Blue Riband at a speed of 30.63 knots. Twice the trophy was reclaimed by the mighty *Normandie*, the great French liner holding the record from March, 1937 until August, 1938, when *Queen Mary* knifed her way west across the Atlantic at 30.99 knots and went home again at 31.69, for twenty-four hours maintaining a sustained average speed of 32.07 knots, a record which stood until July, 1952, when the new United States Lines flagship *United States* set a new official world's record of three days, 10 hours and 40 minutes for an Atlantic crossing.

The *France*, the longest and newest ocean liner in the world, has made no attempt to regain the Blue Riband for her namesake country, relying on spaciousness, elegance, fine food and gracious service to win her share of trans-Atlantic passengers. But the *France*, making her first sailing in 1962, has already confounded the experts who claimed that the era of the gigantic first-class superliner was ended.

Who can say that future queens of the sea, using sources of propulsion as different from the steam turbines of today as they are from the paddle-wheels of 1850, will not sail to meet a new century with a blue pendant streaming proudly from whatever vestidual and streamlined version of a yardarm may remain to them.

FRENCH LINE'S LaBretagne of 1886 (a b o v e) remained in service until 1923, in her later years as **Alesia.**

HOLLAND America Line's third **Statendam**, of 1929, was destroyed in the Nazi bombardment of Rotterdam early in World War II.

STOKEHOLD

THE BOWELS OF THE EARLY twentieth century ocean greyhounds were an inferno of heat, noise and vibration as scores of sweating stokers fed coal to the roaring furnaces . . . sometimes a hundred or more . . . under the massive array of boilers. The coming of the oil-fueled steam turbine and motor liner has changed the engine rooms of present day ships to areas more fit for human habitation.

Chapter Two
PACIFIC
LINERS

Trans-Pacific passenger liner service from the West Coast of the United States had its beginning in 1867, when the Pacific Mail Line began operating side-wheel steamers out of San Francisco. The completion of the first transcontinental railway two years later bolstered the maritime economy of the West Coast and led to the establishment of mail steamer service between San Francisco and Australia by the American-Australian Line. The British liners *Wonga Wonga* and *City of Melbourne*, with the American *Ajax*, inaugurated this service in 1870.

The American-Australian Line was replaced in 1871 by the California, New Zealand & Australia Steam Navigation Co., largely controlled by the pioneer western transportation magnate, Ben Holliday. This company operated the old American side-wheel steamers *Dakota*, *Nevada*, *Nebraska* and *Moses Taylor*. In 1874 the Australasian & American Mail Steamship Co. took over, with the British screw steamers *City of Melbourne, Cyphrenes, Tartar, Mongol, Mikado* and *McGregor*, until the pioneer Pacific Mail Line assumed its operation the following year.

The Oceanic Steamship Company inaugurated San Francisco-Honolulu service in 1882, using chartered vessels until its new liners *Mariposa* and *Alameda* arrived from the builder's yards at Chester, Pennsylvania in 1883. These two ships were destined for long and adventurous careers in West Coast liner service.

By the turn of the century the principal trans-Pacific lines serving the Pacific Coast included the old Pacific Mail Line, operating the liners *City of Peking, City of Rio de Janeiro, China, Korea, Siberia, Manchuria* and *Mongolia*, the Canadian Pacific Railway, with its three lovely, clipper-bowed *Empress* liners out of Vancouver, *Empress of India, Empress of China* and *Empress of Japan* and Occidental & Oriental Steamship Company with the White Star liners *Doric, Coptic* and *Gaelic*. In 1901 the American-Hawaiian Line began service between New York, San Francisco and Hawaii with *American*. The Canadian-Australasian Royal Mail Line had been operating the "All Red Line" Vancouver-Sydney Service since 1893 (after 1901 under ownership of the Union Steamship Company of New Zealand).

In 1903 the maritime world was impressed by the launching of James J. Hill's giant twins, *Minnesota* and *Dakota*, the largest ships ever built in the United States. "Empire Builder" Hill, proprietor of the transcontinental Great Northern Railway, had established his western terminus at Seattle and the big ships were designed to ferry the passengers and freight from his trains across the Pacific to the Orient.

Built to carry tremendous freight loads, as well as a full complement of passengers, the *Minnesota* and *Dakota* exceeded 22,000 tons gross; were driven by 10,000-horsepower reciprocating engines which gave them the moderate cruising speed of 14 knots. They carried 172 first class passengers in true luxury, as well as about eighty cabin class and 1,067 steerage.

The two liners, giants for their time and place, were a source of vast pride to the citizens of Seattle and the Pacific Northwest, but neither of them enjoyed very lucrative or distinguished careers. The *Dakota* ran hard aground on a reef in Yokahama Bay in 1907, finishing herself and the career of her skipper, who spent the remainder of his life as a night watchman in a San Francisco shipyard. The *Minnesota* survived until World War I days, but was plagued by such mechanical and structural difficulties in her later years that her crews claimed she was either being jinxed or sabotaged; possibly both.

In 1901 the Matson Navigation Company was incorporated by Captain William Matson who, since 1882, had been operating a fleet of cargo sailing vessels between San Francisco and Hawaii. Matson Line continued as a "freight only" carrier until 1908,

VENTURA, AND HER SISTER-SHIP SONOMA, were built in 1900 at the Philadelphia yards of William Cramp & Sons for the trans-Pacific service of the Oceanic Line. Twin-screw steel vessels, they were driven by twin triple-expansion steam engines. The somewhat smaller **Sierra,** opposite, served with them on the Pacific.

when its first passenger liner, *Lurline* was delivered. *Lurline* was a 5928-ton single-screw steamer with engines aft, a design which was to characterize Matson Liners until 1927. She had accommodations for only 51 passengers, less than half the capacity of Oceanic's *Alameda* and *Mariposa* and a sixth that of their later *Sierra*, *Sonoma* and *Ventura*, although all of these ships were of the same relative tonnage. Captain Matson was conservative and his first liners were designed as freight carriers first, with the passengers added as a sort of afterthought.

Matson added the *Wilhelmina* in 1909, *Manoa* and *Matsonia* (1) in 1913 and *Maui* in 1917, all with the distinctive "funnel aft" design which has, in recent years, again become popular with the designers of ocean liners.

From 1915 through 1917 the regular lines received a taste of things to come when the Great Northern Pacific Steamship Company (controlled by the Great Northern and Northern Pacific Railways) put its fast liner *Great Northern*, later the *H. F. Alexander*, on a four and a half day express service between Hawaii and San Francisco. However, *Great Northern* was requisitioned by the government at the entry of the United States into World War I, as were *Matsonia*, *Maui* and *Wilhelmina* of Matson and Pacific Mail's

Sierra, *Sonoma* and *Ventura*. During the war years Matson operated the Pacific Coast Steamship Company's coastwise liners *Governor* and *President* on the Honolulu run.

After the war many of the pre-war American flag vessels were replaced by standardized passenger ships of the "502" and "535" class. These ships, built for the U. S. Shipping Board, were approximately 502 and 535 feet in length, with gross tonnages of from ten to fifteen thousand. Equipped with steam turbines and twin-screws, they operated at moderate speed and reasonable economy. For a short time after the war, Matson operated two of them. *President Pierce* and *President Taft* in a service between Baltimore and Hawaii via the Panama Canal, Los Angeles and San Francisco. Within a year, however, the government had assigned these ships, along with the *President Cleveland*, *President Wilson* and *President Lincoln* to the Pacific Mail Line for its trans-Pacific service. In 1926 Matson absorbed the Oceanic Line, operating for some years thereafter as the Matson-Oceanic Steamship Company.

In 1924, octogenarian Robert Dollar inaugurated the famous Dollar Line Around-the-World Service with seven of the wartime-built 502's, *President Harrison*, *President Adams*, *President Garfield*, *President Hayes*,

President Monroe, President Polk, President Van Buren. Two years later Dollar acquired the five 535's which the Pacific Mail Line had been operating. In 1929 he added the old *Manchuria* and *Mongolia* to his fleet, renaming them *President Johnson* and *President Fillmore.*

In addition to the big fleet of 502's and 535's operating from California to the Orient and around the world, the American Mail Line of Seattle maintained regular Oriental sailings from Puget Sound with the 535's *President Jefferson, President Grant, President McKinley, President Jackson* and *President Madison.*

Until the mid-twenties it was virtually certain that anyone taking a deep-sea passenger liner from a West Coast port would board a standardized "502" or "535". The first break in this maritime monotony was brought about by Matson Lines when, in 1927, Cramp shipyards delivered the 17,226-ton *Malolo,* largest and finest ship ever placed in the Hawaiian service. Her 22 knot speed made her the first ship to equal the *Great Northern's* pre-war schedule of four and a half days for the voyage. In 1931, Dollar Lines followed with two new trans-Pacific steamers, *President Coolidge* and *President Hoover,* whose 22,000 tons made them the largest American ships in Pacific service.

The following year Matson, having absorbed the Oceanic Line, brought out two more new liners, *Mariposa* and *Monterey.* These were 22-knot ships with accommodations for more than seven hundred passengers each, and were designed for the San Francisco-Honolulu-Australian service. The next year a third sister, *Lurline* went into service on the San Francisco-Honolulu run with the *Malolo,* now renamed *Matsonia.*

During World War II, all five Matson liners were taken over as transports, leaving the Hawaiian Islands without commercial steamship service throughout the war years.

The Dollar Line had, in the meantime, been taken over by the U. S. Maritime Commission and renamed the American President Lines. The old 502's and 535's were, by the outbreak of the war, largely replaced by new PC-3 class ships, which had been given the old "President" names. They too were diverted to war service and had their share of adventures, as is related in another section of this chapter.

After the war Matson quickly restored island service to an "interim" basis with the *Matsonia,* while the other three liners were scheduled for major overhauls. *Lurline* was completed in 1948, replacing *Matsonia,* which was sold to Panamanian Lines. Work on the others was suspended and they were also sold, the *Monterey* to the United States government and the *Mariposa* to Home Lines, becoming the *Homeric.*

The former Matson Line service to Australia was not resumed after the war and the Hawaiian service was reduced to a one-ship schedule, but in 1954 the

THE YACHT-LIKE EMPRESS LINERS which served the Vancouver-Oriental route at the turn of the century were among the loveliest ships to steam the Pacific.

P. & O.-Orient Line placed a fleet of splendid British flag liners in the Antipodes—West Coast of America service and their surprising success prompted Matson to convert two Mariner type freighters into passenger-cargo liners, rename them *Mariposa* and *Monterey* and place them on that route. The *Monterey* was also repurchased from the government, renamed *Matsonia*,

THE PACIFIC COAST Steamship Company's California - Puget Sound liner **President** was pressed into deep-sea service to cover the West Coast-Hawaiian route during World War I days.
—PUGET SOUND MARITIME HISTORICAL SOCIETY PHOTO

and placed back on the San Francisco-Honolulu run with *Lurline*, thus restoring weekly sailings.

In addition to the entry of British P & O liners in the trans-Pacific service, the American companies saw brief post-war periods of new competition in the Hawaiian trade. In 1953-54, the Hawaiian-Pacific Line went into business with the venerable steamer *Aleutian*, formerly a coastwise liner of the Alaska Steamship Company on the Seattle-Alaska route. A ship of only 6,361 tons and then almost half a century old, she was no match for the *Lurline* and was soon dispatched to the scrapyard.

More serious competition was provided by the Hawaiian Steamship Company, owned by Hawaiian Textron, Inc., with its *Leilani*, wartime-built as the transport *General W. P. Richardson;* later the *La-Guardia.* However, *Leilani* also failed to take sufficient patronage away from the well-established Matson Liners and she ended service in 1958. Following a complete conversion at the yards of Puget Sound Bridge & Dry Dock Company in Seattle, she entered American President Lines service in 1962 as the *President Roosevelt.*

Today the prospective ocean voyager from West Coast ports enjoys a choice of fine ships . . . the

THE LITTLE MARIPOSA led a long and adventurous life on both trans-Pacific and coastwise routes in the Pacific.

trim white Matson Liners, the handsome new President ships of American President Lines, and the great post-war British liners of the P & O.

The Pacific liners have not quite attained the size and speed of the highest class of North Atlantic express steamers, but they are, in some instances, approaching that standard. Certainly they have come a long way from the creaking wooden side-wheelers of the nineteenth century Pacific Mail Line.

COASTWISE LINER Queen of the Pacific, her name later shortened to **Queen,** also made blue-water voyages to the Hawaiian Islands.
—MARINE HISTORY OF PACIFIC NORTHWEST PHOTO

The American President Lines Role in World War II

by

EUGENE F. HOFFMAN,

Vice President, American President Lines

As a result of the war in Europe in September 1939, regular trades and services of many Allied Nations in competition with American President Lines were either disrupted or completely suspended. In order to offset this serious loss of ship tonnage and at the same time cope with the abnormally heavy movement of critical strategic materials and the general cargo movement, American President lines, through various charter and agency agreements, supplemented its own ship tonnage with vessels of other American flag owner. This supplemental tonnage was placed on the American President Lines' vital routes between this country and China, Philippines, Netherlands Indies, Malaya, Burma, India and Ceylon. Thus prior to Pearl Harbor, American President Lines, in addition to its own vessels, were operating agents for ships owned or controlled by:

American Pioneer Line
Coastwise—Far East Line
Baltimore Mail Line
Lykes Brothers Steamship Company
Luckenbach Steamship Company

THE ALAMEDA WAS MARIPOSA'S old running-mate on the Oceanic deep-water Pacific service, later joined her in coastwise passenger service between Seattle and Alaska. She survived several standings in Pacific waters (below) and was finally destroyed by fire while laid up at Seattle in the early 1930's.

—JOE WILLIAMSON PHOTO

U. S. Army Transport Service

U. S. Maritme Commission (Danish Ships)

While the majority of these ships were freighters, which during 1940 and eleven months of 1941 were pouring essential raw materials into the United States, the big passenger carriers, such as the *Presidents Coolidge, Pierce, Cleveland* and *Taft* were shuttling back and forth across the Pacific, bringing home capacity loads of evacuees and refugees. On their outward voyages these same vessels were carrying Army and Navy personnel and needed supplies to bases overseas. General MacArthur and his staff originally sailed to Manila on the *President Coolidge.*

Meanwhile, American President Lines' Round-World vessels were bringing into Atlantic Coast U. S. ports similar capacity loads of evacuees from Mediterranean ports and war-torn Europe.

JIM HILL'S HUGE cargo-passenger liner **Dakota** (opposite) and her sister-ship, **Minnesota,** were the largest American-built ships of their time. Operating between Seattle and the Orient, they were the pride of the Pacific Northwest at the beginning of the twentieth century. **Dakota** foundered after ramming a reef in Yokahama Bay in 1907. —SEATTLE HISTORICAL SOCIETY PHOTO

When on December 8, 1941, Japan formally declared war on the United States and Great Britain, the steamer *President Harrison* which had previously delivered a complement of United States Marines at Manila, was on her way back to Chinwangtao, North China to evacuate additional Marines from Peking. The *President Harrison* was overhauled by Japanese naval units off Woosung and seized as a prize of war. When the Captain and crew saw that capture was inevitable, they risked their lives by running the ship hard aground on a rocky island in the East China Sea, deliberately wrecking the vessel in order to render her useless to the Japanese. Her crew was interned and all officers and passengers aboard with naval or military ratings were transferred to prison camps. Thus, the *President Harrison* became the first gold star in American President Lines Service Flag for floating equipment lost.

After the die was cast at Pearl Harbor, the entire physical resources and facilities of the American President Lines, plus the experience and energy of the management and personnel, were placed at the disposal of the United States Government and con-

FORERUNNER OF SHIPS TO COME, early Matson Hawaiian liners like the **Maui** were built with engines and funnels aft, a design which has become popular with marine architects of the 1960's.
—MATSON LINES PHOTO

secrated to the task of winning the war at the earliest possible moment.

Upon creation of War Shipping Administration, all company-owned vessels were bareboat chartered thereto, and key members of American President Lines' staff and special training in the shipping business were made available to the War Shipping Administration for important overseas assignment. Some APL staff members were already on loan to the government in such positions as administrator for China Defense Supplies Corporation and Lend-Lease in India and Burma.

Three American President Lines vessels were in or near Manila when the bombs fell on December 8. These were the: S. S. *Ruth Alexander*, S. S. *President Grant* and S. S. *President Madison*.

The *Ruth Alexander* and the *Grant* were in port in Manila when the shooting started. There they became the principal target for aerial bombardment.

The Navy notified company officials that they would not be able to give protection to ships in Manila Harbor and suggested that it would be safer

for the vessels to "make a run for it." After consultation with the Masters it was decided to sail. Consequently, under cover of darkness, both ships departed.

The *President Grant*, under command of Captain W. S. Tyrrell, made good her escape and after an exciting and eventful voyage made safe port in Australia.

The *Ruth Alexander* under command of Captain F. P. Willarts, was not so fortunate. She escaped at night, some time after the *President Grant* departed, but was caught by Japanese bombers in the Celebes Sea off Balikpapan. Defenseless against the merciless bombing, the gallant little steamer was blasted to the bottom of the sea, and so became gold star No. 2 in the company service flag. One member of her crew was killed and a half dozen others were wounded. After tossing about in open boats for many hours, survivors were sighted and picked up by a Dutch Dornier flying boat and taken to Balikpapan.

The rescue was heroic. The Dutch pilot of the Dornier ordered all his bombs and supplies jettisoned

56

STANDARDIZED PASSENGER LINERS of the "502" and "535" classes, built for the shipping board during World War I, dominated the rosters of American flag lines on the Pacific for several years after the war. This one was the American Mail Lines' **President McKinley** which operated between Seattle and the Orient. **President Jefferson** of the same line is shown on the following pages.
—JOE WILLIAMSON PHOTO

to make room for the 46-man crew of the sunken vessel. At that, the only way this number could be accommodated was to have them stand close together, like sticks of cordwood. Even the wounded had to stand straight up. The plane's load was so heavy the pilot had to taxi five miles before he could get his ship into the air.

The SS *President Madison*, commanded by Captain Valdemar Nielsen, was south of the Philippines when the war broke out. This vessel played hide and seek, through the Dutch East Indies, sailing mostly at night, and eventually made home port safely.

When the SS *President Taylor* sailed from San Francisco January 5, 1941, it marked the 17th anniversary of the inauguration of the company's famous 'Round-World service. In 17 years "President" liners, sailing every two weeks westward from San Francisco, had completed more than 350 circumnavigations totaling 10,000,000 miles. This record had been achieved without loss of a single passenger's life as a result of accident.

But even before the 17th anniversary was celebrated, events were happening that were to jeopardize that famous route of the 'round-world ships. The great Mediterranean Sea, an important segment of the circuit, was being claimed by Italy's Il Duce as "mare nostrum." The hazards of the war were increasing constantly and although American President Lines used the Mediterranean route as long as possible, it finally became necessary for it to abandon the regular course and route its vessels from the Far East around the Cape of Good Hope, a deviation of more than 3,000 miles which lengthened the voyage by some 10 days additional steaming, a serious matter when speed was vital in building up the nation's stock pile of strategic material.

An example of how American imports of these materials jumped during 1941 is offered in the statistics of crude rubber. Prior to 1940, America imported an average of 400,000 tons of rubber per annum. In 1941, rubber imports exceeded on million tons, a substantial portion of which was carried in ships owned or operated by American President Lines. Comparable increases reflected in the figures for tin and other war-making commodities.

After the Neutrality Act was repealed, American

DEATH OF A BRAVE SHIP: The P & O liner **Rawalpindi** steams in with blazing guns to fight the German battle cruisers **Scharnhorst** and **Gneisenau.** (See **The Liners at War,** page 146).

IN HAPPIER DAYS

RAWALPINDI, BUILT IN 1925, was a favorite among the Indian mail liners of the P & O's post-World War I fleet. Her interior fittings were in the grand tradition of dark-panelled elegance. At lower left is pictured her lavishly appointed first class Music Room; below, right, a **cabine de luxe** on **Rawalpindi** was, indeed, de luxe.

—STEWART BALE PHOTOS, LIVERPOOL

MATSON LINES' MARIPOSA of pre-World War II days is now in service on the Atlantic under the Panamanian flag as the Home Line's **Homeric.**

—MATSON LINES PHOTO

OPPOSITE PAGE: Although the Matson Liner **Matsonia** normally sails from San Francisco directly for Honolulu, this picture was taken in Seattle during a recent special voyage via that port.

—JOE WILLIAMSON PHOTO

President Lines, along with many other American steamship companies, diverted much of its tonnage to carrying Lend-Lease cargoes to the Red Sea, and to Murmansk and Archangel.

With America's formal entry into the war, this famous 'Round-World service, like the Company's trans-Pacific service, was completely disrupted, and all APL tonnage then became consolidated in the newly formed War Shipping Administration pool.

In the Summer of 1941, due to mounting tension and repeated hostile actions of Japanese toward American and British nations in China, American President Lines moved its Far Eastern headquarters from Shanghai to Manila. Already the company had discontinued steamer calls at Japanese ports, first curtailing them and finally bypassing Japan entirely.

The headquarters staff, then under the direction of Vice President Oscar G. Steen, arrived in Manila in late August, 1941, and in January, 1942, all staff members, except four who had previously joined the U.S. Armed Forces, were interned at Santo Tomas prison,

Manila. Of the four APL employees who "joined up," one was reported killed in action, a second drowned when a Japanese prison ship went down, and the other two were interned by the Japanese.

The company's Singapore staff escaped by plane to Java, and eventually made their way to Australia.

The Hong Kong staff was interned in Stanley Prison for a period of six months and then repatriated on the first *Gripsholm* to America.

Although the headquarters office had been removed from Shanghai, a skeleton crew had been retained there to look after the company's interest. This staff was not immediately imprisoned but was confined to a restricted area in the International Settlement. However, in February, 1943, the Shanghai staff members were placed in various prison camps. In September, 1943, three of them were repatriated to the U.S. Three others remained in internment.

In September, 1943, three of the staff at Manila were also repatriated, leaving fourteen still interned there.

Creation of the War Shipping Administration

EXOTIC ESCORT: In contrast to the usual tugboat escort is the flotilla of Polynesian outriggers which greets the 18,564-ton Matson Hawaiian cruise liner **Lurline** at termination of San Francisco-Honolulu voyage, above. S.S. **Mariposa**, below, provides Matson trans-Pacific service in company with her sister, **Monterey.** She's pictured here heading down the Willamette River at Portland, accompanied by the big Port of Portland stern-wheeler **Portland** and Shaver Transportation Company's towboat **Capt. George** following her reconstruction by the Willamette Iron & Steel Co.

—MATSON LINES PHOTO

brought a demand for experienced shipping executives to serve the Administration at various world ports. No less than ten American President Lines officials were loaned to the Government for this purpose. They served at Allied control ports in India, South America, Europe, Australia, Hawaii and various ports in continental United States.

In addition to these men with the War Shipping Administration, American President Lines had 131 of its regular shoreside staff serving with the Armed Forces — Army, Navy and Marine Corps.

In the meantime, American President Lines, in common with other U.S. merchant ship operators, was receiving its full share of Liberty ships and others that began sliding down the ways in ever increasing numbers in our nation's shipyards.

At the time over eighty vessels had been assigned to American President Lines as agents for the War Shipping Administration. However, from December 7, 1941, cargo operations on various other vessels assigned to Army, Navy and Lend-Lease, for which American President Lines also acted as agent, ran well into the hundreds of ships.

Contrast this picture with American President Lines' normal peacetime operation of less than 20 vessels, and one begins to appreciate the enormity of the wartime operation.

And like any other phase of modern warfare, the operation of so many units of equipment implies a certain ratio of casualty. American President Lines had its share, and its log books and other Company records are replete with accounts of marine disaster and glowing tributes to the heroism and expert seamanship of officers and men.

The company's pre-war fleet consisted of these vessels:

7 Old 'Round-the-World "502s"
7 New 'Round-the-World "C3Ps"
1 Luxury passenger liner—*President Coolidge*
3 Trans-Pacific "535s" (*Cleveland—Pierce—Taft*)
1 SS *President Johnson* (then 37 years old)
1 SS *Ruth Alexander* (former Pacific Coast Passenger Carrier)

Of these 20 vessels, only the old *President Johnson*

THIS COMPOSITE PHOTOGRAPH pictures three of the American President Lines' handsome trans-Pacific passenger liners, **President Cleveland, President Wilson** and **President Hoover.** The **Hoover** was formerly the **Panama** of the two-ship government owned Panama line, sister-ship to the **Ancon,** lower right, which is now the school ship **State of Maine.**

—AMERICAN PRESIDENT LINES PHOTO

(which had advanced in age to 42 years), and two C3Ps, the SS *President Polk* and the SS *President Monroe*, were returned to the company.

It is a stirring testimonial to the American Way that within a period of little more than a decade this humble fleet of three war-weary ships could evolve into the mighty merchant armada that now fans out over four major world trade routes under the American President Lines' flag.

Like the winning of the war itself, this notable achievement of building a peace-time merchant fleet would not have been possible without the 3-way partnership of government, private industry and labor—all working together for the common good.

THE ALEUTIAN, BUILT IN 1906 as the **Mexico,** went into Alaska Steamship service between Seattle and the Far North in 1930 after years of service on the Atlantic; with the suspension of Alaska Line passenger service in 1954 she was purchased by the short-lived Caribbean-Atlantic Lines, given a coat of white paint, a swimming pool and a new name, **Tradewinds.** She bravely tried the Hawaiian and Caribbean cruise business, but was better fitted for sailing the kind of cool waters pictured below. She soon ended up in a Japanese scrapyard.

Southern Cross, 20,204 tons, 1955

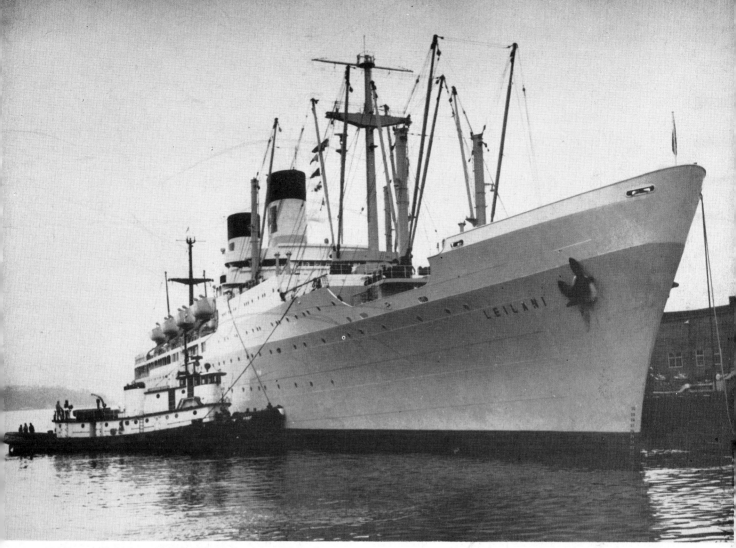

MORE SERIOUS COMPETITION was given established lines in Hawaiian service when the Hawaiian Textron Company placed the big **Leilani** in tourist class service to the Islands. Earlier in her career she was the **LaGuardia,** sailing for some time to Israeli ports under the American Export Lines' houseflag. Now virtually a new ship after a multi-million dollar rebuilding, she's the American President Lines' **President Roosevelt.**

—JOE WILLIAMSON PHOTO

S.S. PRESIDENT HOOVER, below, steams out of San Francisco Bay in Dollar Lines Pacific service. Later taken over by American President Lines, she and her sister-ship **President Coolidge** were lost during World War II service.

—WILLIAMS PHOTOGRAPHY, SAN FRANCISCO

YAWATA MARU, 558-foot N.Y.K. liner of 16,500 tons, was built in 1939, just in time to become a casualty of World War II.

S.S. MIIKE MARU of the Nippon Yusen Kaisha arrived at Seattle in August, 1896, inaugurating Japanese flag steamship service between the Orient and the West Coast of the United States. N.Y.K. passenger steamers and motor liners served the Seattle-Orient route until September, 1960, when the **Hikawa Maru** made her final eastward voyage. —SEATTLE HISTORICAL SOCIETY PHOTO

CERAMIC, 15,896 tons, 1948

ASAMA MARU, above, and 560-foot **Tatsuta Maru**, built in 1929 were, at over 16,900 tons, largest Japanese passenger liners. In peacetime NYK service, **Asama Maru** acted as "opposite number" to Swedish liner **Gripsholm** in exchange of noncombatant repatriates between United States and Japan after Pearl Harbor. Like all other Japanese liners except NYK's **Hikawa Maru**, lower right, she was lost during the war. **Hikawa Maru**, serving as a hospital ship, was spared to resume Orient-Puget Sound service until her retirement in 1960. Now she's a floating hotel in Japan, as pictured below.
—JOE WILLIAMSON PHOTO

横浜市教育委員会推薦
神奈川県観光協会推薦

海の教室

氷川丸

見る船・泊まれる船

The Hikawamaru Co., Ltd.

P & O-ORIENT LINES' ORCADES is one of the splendid new ships placed in service in recent years. Like **Arcadia**, opposite page, pictured as she was being eased into her Seattle berth in 1961, **Orcades** operates in P & O's long-haul service between Vancouver, California ports and the Antipodes by way of Hawaii and the Orient. Below, the author, representing the Seattle Port Commission, presents a Northwest Indian totem carving to Captain Charles W. Mayne of **Arcadia** during the liner's 1961 visit there. At 29,734 tons, **Arcadia** is the largest liner ever to call at that port.

—JOE WILLIAMSON COLLECTION

Below: **S.S. SANTA ROSA**, Grace Lines.

INAUGURATING "EXPRESS TRAIN SERVICE between the Pacific Northwest and San Francisco. James J. Hill's notable coastwise liner **Great Northern,** later the **H. F. Alexander** of the Pacific Steamship Co., is pictured on her maiden voyage arrival at Flavel, Oregon, northern terminus of the Hill steamships.

S.S. Great Northern-Flavel Or.

PRIDE OF THE BRITISH MERCHANT NAVY on the Pacific is P & O's giant new flagship, the revolutionary **Canberra.**

—P & O-ORIENT LINES PHOTO

SAILING of paddle-steamer **Hindustan,** left, September 24, 1842, inaugurated P & O mail service to India. **Hindustan,** of over 2,000 tons, was then the largest liner in the world, but she could be carried on the sports deck of the **Canberra** without crowding things much.

ABOVE: FIRST CLASS DINING SALON, S.S. Canberra, is happy combination of traditional P & O elegance with modern decor. Next lower: "Pop-Inn" aboard **Canberra** is teen-age haven where soft drink dispenser and juke box are provided. Special facilities for small children have long been available on first-class liners, but public rooms designed to teen-age specifications are a recent development.

BELOW: THE WALLS of this first class two-bed cabin on **Canberra** are covered with Vynide, a soft plastic of linen like texture. Plain dark bedspreads are brightened by orange and blue pillows, and orange dominates the textured silk curtains. The furniture is light elm and a charcoal carpet covers the floor. Lower left, first class cabin on **Oriana.**

—P & O-ORIENT LINES PHOTO

PRESIDENT FILLMORE, below, in American
President Lines service at the outbreak of
World War II, was the old Pacific Mail Liner
Mongolia, built at Camden, N.J. in 1903.

Return of the Washington Volunteer's from Manila on the Pennsylvania Oct 9th 1899

BUILT AT Philadelphia in 1873 for the Inman (later American) Line, the **Pennsylvania,** with her sister-ships **Ohio, Illinois** and **Indiana** were the first trans-Atlantic steamers to be built in the United States since pre-Civil War days. In later years they served as Spanish War troopships and in Alaska Gold Rush service. **Pennsylvania** is shown here returning the Washington Volunteer Regiment from Manila to Seattle in 1899.

—SEATTLE HISTORICAL SOCIETY PHOTO

LATEST PRESIDENT LINER . . . S.S. **President Roosevelt** steams past Seattle World's Fair Space Needle as she leaves the building yards of Puget Sound Bridge & Dry Dock Company April 17, 1962. Built at Kearney, N.J. in 1944 as the military transport **General W. P. Richardson,** she underwent a ten million dollar reconversion job at the Seattle shipbuilding company, emerging as virtually a new ship. She now has completely air-conditioned luxury accommodations for 450 passengers in trans-Pacific cruise service to Far East ports.

—PUGET SOUND BRIDGE & DRYDOCK CO. PHOTO

CAPTAIN K. A. AHLIN inaugurated famous Dollar Line round-the-world service when he took S.S. **President Harrison** through the Golden Gate on January 5, 1924. Modern American President Liners still follow the trail he blazed four decades ago.

—SEATTLE HISTORICAL SOCIETY PHCTO

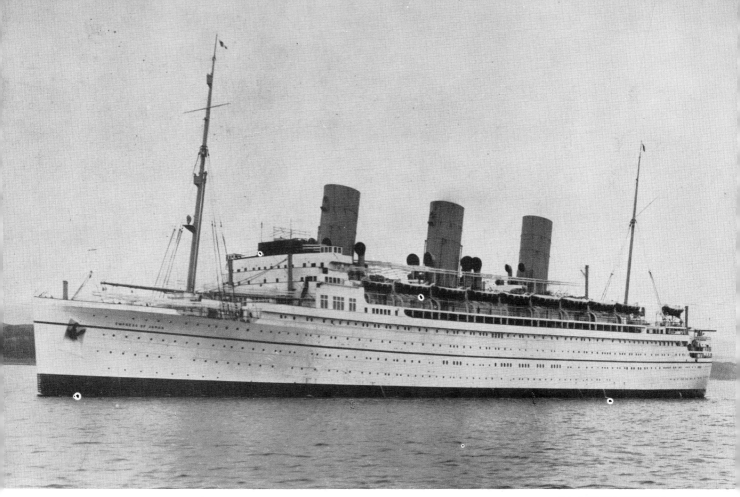

R. M. S. MARAMA,

Chapter Three

DOWN UNDER

● S.S. "ORSOVA"

Passenger ship service between Great Britain and the Commonwealth nations of South Africa, Australia and New Zealand began in the age of sail, many years before the first scheduled liners dispatched from the Pacific Coast ports of the United States to the seas "down under." Some of the lines still prominent in the trade between the British Isles and the Antipodes trace their beginnings to clipper ship days.

By the turn of the century, however, the coal-burning passenger steamships were in command of the vast waterways of the Southern Hemisphere. The Shaw Savill Line had combined with the Albion Line two decades earlier. The combined sailing fleets of the two companies, which had served Australia and New Zealand since the 1850's were sold; the proceeds invested in two new steel steamers. Built by Denny's of Dumbarton, the *Arawa* and *Tainui* were single-screw, two funnelled four-masted bark-rigged liners with clipper bows and beautiful lines, each of more than five thousand tons register. Capable of speeds of 15 knots (the crack North Atlantic liners were averaging 18 knots on their short voyages), the *Arawa* and *Tainui* offered accommodations of a kind never before seen on the remote seas they sailed . . . including bathrooms and electric lights in all three classes. They carried 95 first-class passengers, 52 second-class and from 200 to 700 in the steerage.

The *Arawa* and *Tainui* were joined by the former White Star Atlantic liners *Ionic*, *Doric* and *Coptic* to provide monthly round-the-world steam service, going out by Cape Town and Tasmania and returning by Cape Horn, Montevideo and Rio.

In 1901 three big new liners were added to the fleet, the Belfast Yard of Harland and Wolff launching the *Athenic*, *Corinthic* and *Ionic* to join the *Gothic*, also turned out by Harland and Wolff. The development of passenger vessels in this trade was becoming almost as dramatic as that on the North Atlantic. The *Gothic*, at 7,755 tons, had been the largest ship ever to use the Port of London or engaged in the Australian trade. The three liners which followed her all exceeded 12,000 tons.

The legendary P & O had dispatched its first steam liner, the wooden bark-rigged *Chusan*, in 1842. By 1900 the long, low, two-funneled liners of the P & O, with their black, white-striped hulls, ships like the *Britannia*, *India* and *Egypt*, were furrowing the eastern seas from Bombay to Sydney.

The mail steamers of the Union Steamship Company of New Zealand, resplendent with their brilliant green, gold-banded hulls and crimson funnels, covered sea routes from New Zealand and Australia to the South Sea Islands and north to Vancouver, on the West Coast of Canada.

The beautiful lavender-hulled *Castle* liners of the Castle Mail Steamship Company were sailing from Southampton to Madeira, Cape Town, Port Elizabeth and Durban; from London and Plymouth to Las Palmas, Teneriffe, Ascension, St. Helena, Cape Town, Lourenco Marques and Beira. The graceful, clipper-bowed *Marathon* and *Miltiades* in the green, white and buff colors of the Aberdeen & Commonwealth Line were setting the pace for future long-haul liners with their 35-day voyages from London to Melbourne by way of Cape Town.

Like the Atlantic lines, the fleets of these companies suffered grievous losses during the first World War. (56 P & O Liners alone were sunk by torpedo; one, the *Trewyn,* lost without trace). The immediate post-war period was devoted to fleet replacement programs. Orient Steam Navigation Company, subsidiary of P & O, brought out its famous class of 20,000-ton, two-funnelled turbine liners, *Otranto, Oronsay, Orford, Orama* and *Orontes*, all launched between 1924 and 1929, while P & O built its first turbine steamer, *Mongolia* and the handsome turbo-electric twin screw *Viceroy of India.* (All but three of these World War I replacement liners were lost by enemy action in World War II. The *Orontes* and *Otranto* survived to be scrapped in recent years, the *Orontes*, the last of them, in Spain in 1962-63). The old *Mongolia* is now the "new" Mexican merchant marine flagship *Acapulco.*

Laid down at about the same time as the "O" ships were four smaller P & O "R" Class liners of 16,700

S.S. NORTHERN STAR, above, 24,733-ton turbine liner, is newest passenger ship of Shaw Savill fleet, was launched June 27, 1961 by Her Majesty Queen Elizabeth and placed in service the following year, making four round-the world voyages yearly from Southampton. She has a capacity of 1,412 passengers in all-tourist class accomodations. **Gothic,** 15,911 tons, below left, was commissioned Royal Yacht to carry the Queen and Duke of Edinburgh on their Commonwealth Tour of 1953-54.

—SHAW SAVILL LINE PHOTO

tons, equipped with reciprocating engines (the conservative P & O had been reluctant to adopt turbine propulsion), *Ranpura, Rajputana, Ranchi* and the gallant *Rawalpindi,* which went down with guns blazing against the German battleship *Deutschland* in the early months of World War II. These four were scaled-down versions of the big 21,000-ton *Maloja* and *Mooltan,* first big post-war P & O Liners to be completed (in 1923), also driven by quadruple-expansion engines and splendid looking vessels in the classic ocean liner tradition, with massive, raked funnels and tall masts.

Having once parted with tradition, with the turbine-driven *Mongolia* of 1922 and the *Viceroy of India,* first turbine-electric deep-sea liner in the world, P & O went all the way with their next ships, the "beautiful twins," *Strathaird* and *Strathnaver.* These sleek, three-funnelled 24,000-ton liners were not only powered with turbo-electric drive which gave them a top speed of 23 knots, but even departed from the venerable company color scheme of black hulls and funnels and stone-colored upperworks. The first *Straths,* like those which followed them, were georgeous in all-white paint and yellow funnels.

The *Strathaird* and *Strathnaver* of 1931 were followed by the *Strathmore* in 1935 and *Stratheden* and *Strathallan* in 1937, similar ships, but equipped with a single funnel amidships rather than the splendid three of the first *Straths.* Ocean liner buffs were saddened when the *Strathaird* and *Strathnaver* were also reduced to a single stack each in the course of post-World War II reconversion from troopship duty, but the age of the three and four-funnelled liners was past. Just as early twentieth centry voyagers counted the stacks and rated the prestige of the ship accordingly,

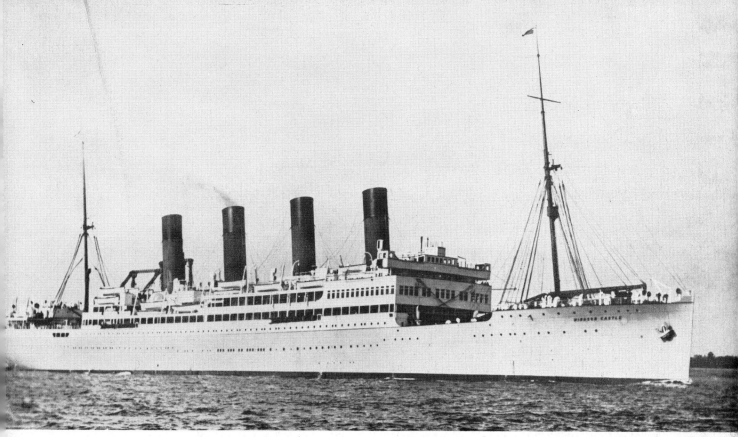

THE CHANGES OF FOUR DECADES in ship styling are reflected in these photographs of Union - Castle's second and third **Windsor Castles.** The 18,967-ton **Windsor Castle** of 1922, above, and her sister-ship **Arundel Castle** were the first of the line's post-World War I ships and the last steamers to be built until after the second World War. Their four tall funnels, lofty masts and straight stems were typical of their era. (In 1937-38 they were lengthened and extensively rebuilt; given two smaller funnels and raked bows).

—UNION-CASTLE LINE PHOTO

THE NEW WINDSOR CASTLE, below, of 38,000 tons, was build by Cammell Laird & Company, entering service in 1960. Like the older **Windsor Castle,** she's a twin-screw turbine steamer, but her shaft horsepower of 45,000 gives her a top speed of over 25 knots (service speed 22½), compared to the 17 of the older ship. Not as revolutionary in appearance as some of the other newest super-liners, **Windsor Castle's** handsomely streamlined profile is a satisfying blend of the modern and traditional in ship design, a comfort to those who think a ship should look like a ship.

—UNION-CASTLE LINE PHOTO

mid-century travelers, in a more sophisticated age, looked upon too many funnels as an indication of primitive design.

The P & O entered a dramatic new era after the second World War, having lost almost a million and a quarter tons of shipping in that holocaust. It began with the commissioning of *Arcadia* in 1953 and her sister-ship *Iberia* in 1954. The gross tonnage of *Arcadia* is 29,734, her 42,500-horsepower engines give her a service speed of 22½ knots and she provides luxury accommodations for 1,400 passengers. The *Iberia* is of similar specifications.

Then, in 1956, P & O laid down the largest ship to be built in Great Britain in two decades, the fastest ship ever to steam the Pacific-Australian trade routes and the largest turbo-electric ship in the world; the great *Canberra* of more than 45,000 tons.

In appearance *Canberra* is a shock to lovers of traditional ships, for she breaks all the traditional rules. Her engines, like those of the early Matson Liners, are

BALMORAL CASTLE and her sister-ship Edinburgh Castle, twin-screw quadruple-expansion steamers were typical of the pre-motorship era of the Union-Castle Mail Steamship Company, Ltd. Built in 1910, these 13,300-ton steamers served in the line's mail service out of Southampton.

right aft. The ancient association of power with funnels has been completely abandoned. The slender wing-like structure at the stern which vents her boilers has no resemblance to a ship's funnel. Her single mast, which rises from a streamlined tower of bridge structures has lost all family resemblance to the sail-rigged wooden masts of the early liners. Her lifeboats, always crowning a liner's upper deck, have been stowed in alcoves below decks.

There are crotchety old-timers who will tell you *Canberra* is a maritime monstrosity, not to be mentioned in the same breath with such sea queens of the past as *Mauretania* and *Aquitania*, or even the

BELOW: DOMINION MONARCH passing clipper Cutty Sark, 1939.

—SHAW SAVILL LINE PHOTO

Queen Mary, last of the great liners to be built on classic lines. But practical shipping men will tell you she is twenty years ahead of the existing Atlantic giants, not only in date of construction, but in conception. Her passenger spaces sweep forward from the engine room bulkhead at the stern, unencumbered all the way. The topmost of her 13 decks is clean and free of all obstructions. Her superstructure is of aluminum and she is completely air-conditioned.

Shaw, Savill and Albion also departed from the age of coal-burning steamers with reciprocating engines in its post-World War I rebuilding program, but this line moved in the direction of the diesel motor, rather than turbo-electric steam drive, as did the Union-Castle Line.

The first Shaw-Savill motor liners, *Coptic, Karamea* and *Taranaki,* were small ships of 8,300 tons, but they performed well and were followed by larger ones, climaxed, in 1939, with the commissioning of *Dominion Monarch,* a unique 27,000-ton passenger motorship built by Swan, Hunter & Wigham Richardson, the largest British merchant ship built on the Tyne since the *Mauretania* of 1907. Her four 8,000-horsepower Doxford opposed-piston diesels, directly connected to quadruple screws, made her the most powerful motor-

EYE OF THE DAWN was the English translation of this handsome liner's Maori name, **Awatea.** A 13,482-ton turbine steamer, built by Vickers Armstrong at Barrow in 1936, her service speed of 22 knots, which she could easily exceed, made her the third fastest ship in the British Merchant Navy. Designed for the intercolonial (Australia-New Zealand) service of the Union Steamship Co. of New Zealand, she made several trans-Pacific runs for "All Red Route" to Vancouver. Requisitioned as a trooper, and later converted to an assault landing ship, she was bombed and sunk during the North African invasion of 1942.

—JOE WILLIAMSON COLLECTION

ship in the world. In addition to carrying over five hundred passengers in all first-class accommodations, *Dominion Monarch* was fitted out to carry a half-million cubic feet of refrigerated cargo.

Union-Castle built only two steamships after World War I, *Windsor Castle* and *Arundel Castel,* in 1922. Originally these 19,000-ton turbine liners were equipped with no less than four tall funnels each, but in 1937 they were reconditioned and lengthened and the four tall, thin funnels replaced by two short, fat ones.

Carnarvon Castle of 1926 was the first of the line's motorships. The big *Capetown Castle,* launched in 1937, was the largest motor liner in the "down under" trade, at 27,001 tons, until the arrival of *Dominion Monarch* in 1939, rated at 27,155. The two ships shared the honors by this narrow margin until after World War II, when *Dominion Monarch* was extensively overhauled and remeasured. Her new tonnage was listed at 26,473, giving the Union-Castle Liner the lead again

Both companies have now returned to steam engines in their more recent vessels. In 1947 Shaw-Savill took delivery of the first of a quartette of notable twin-

screw, turbine passenger-cargo liners, which were given the names of former White Star Liners operated by Shaw-Savill. The 560-foot *Corinthic* and *Athenic* were followed, in 1948, by *Ceramic* and *Gothic.* *Gothic,* in 1951, received the rare honor of being commissioned a Royal Yacht to carry King George V, Queen Elizabeth, and Princess Margaret on the Royal Commonwealth Tour scheduled for that year. The death of the King cancelled that voyage, but the following year she carried the Queen and Duke of Edinburgh on their Commonwealth Tour, commanded by

TYPICAL BAY CLASS LINER of Aberdeen & Commonwealth Line, a Shaw Savill subsidiary.

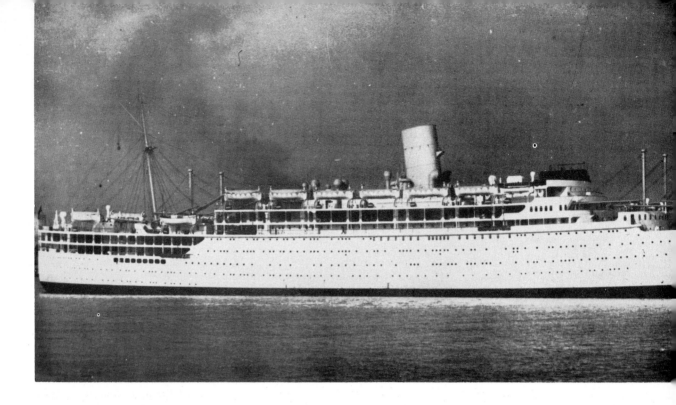

THE HANDSOME STRATH LINERS, like **Strathmore,** above, and **Strathnaver,** lower right, marked the entry of the traditionally conservative P & O into the era of turbo-electric luxury liners. After World War II service, **Strathnaver** lost two of her three funnels in refitting and more close resembled the newer **Strathmore.** They ended their service in 1961 and 1962 respectively.

—P & O-ORIENT LINES PHOTO

the line's commodore, Captain David Aitchison, formerly of the *Dominion Monarch.* The line's latest passenger liners, *Southern Cross* and *Northern Star* are,

ARAWA and TAINUI, 1887

DOMINION MONARCH, 1939

like the new P & O Liners, of radical design, with engines aft in the style pioneered by Captain William Matson (although his design was aimed at convenience of cargo-handling, rather than uncluttered comfort for passengers).

The Union Steamship Company of New Zealand is still accurately named, since its fleet is largely steam-powered, but it was the first shipping line to place a large motor passenger liner in trans-oceanic service. Its *Aorangi,* built by Fairfield in 1924, was a 17,491-ton vessel powered by quadruple screw, two-cycle single-acting Sulzer Diesels. She served the old "All Red" Vancouver-Sydney route, after 1931 in a joint operation with the Canadian Pacific under the title of the Canadian-Australasian Line, for many pre-war years. After World War II she returned to her old route, where she remained until she went to the scrappers in 1953, ending the British service which had begun in 1893.

Although the much longer distances involved in sailing the Pacific trade routes have made impractical the brief, high-speed dashes of the crack Atlantic liners, it is clear that in advanced design, in comfort and even in size, the passenger liners that ply the mighty waters of the Pacific are fast coming to rival the traditional sea queens of the Atlantic.

Chapter Four

THE LINES

To the confirmed ship-watcher (and they are as dedicated a band as the inland bird-watchers) much of the fascination of their avocation lies in the ability to identify the line or company to which a ship belongs by the distinctive colors and insignia of the various fleets.

Sometimes these distinctions are undiscernable to the lay eye, but the practiced ship-watcher has no difficulty in spotting the minute variations. The old White Star Liners, for instance, had a color scheme most similar to that of the affiliated Shaw-Savill Line, but the true ship-watcher could tell you the difference at a distance of four sea miles. The stripe around the black hulls of the White Star ships was gold; on the

Shaw-Savill Liners white. The buff funnels of Shaw-Savill steamers had a bit more pink in the paint mixture, and the crows-nests on the foremasts of White Star ships were painted white, while Shaw-Savill specifications called for mast-brown.

On the North Atlantic the black and white French Line ships with their black-topped crimson funnels are frequently mistaken for Cunard Liners, but even an apprentice ship-watcher can spot the three narrow black stripes below the black band which identifies the British ships.

A few passenger lines have colors so distinctive that there can be no doubt as to the ownership of their vessels. The almost heliotrope hulls of the Union-Castle Liners make them easy to identify, even though their red and black funnels are similar to those of the French Liners. The Union Steamship Company of New Zealand Liners have funnels almost identical to Cunard's, but the brilliant green, gold-striped hulls make them easy to identify.

The P & O gave ship-watchers a bit of trouble when the white-hulled *Strathnaver* and *Strathaird* arrived on the scene, for their white hulls and three bright buff funnels gave them a strong resemblance to the C.P.R. *Empress* liners of the day. It was soon noted, however, that the *Straths* had red boot-topping; the *Empresses* green. Since then the P & O has adopted a deep cream color for its hulls, while the Canadian Pacific ships now sport the company's red and white checked house-flag on their stacks.

The increasing popularity of white as the basic hull color for passenger liners has also made things more difficult for the ship-watcher. (In the past, the hulls of regular line-service ships were often painted white when they were placed on cruise service, and it was found that interior temperatures remained several degrees cooler when they wore their sun-reflecting white).

In this uniform age, even the ocean liners are losing much of the unique "personalities" of the older ships. The Bibby Liners were the last hold-outs, those modern motor liners with the tall pink funnel and four lofty masts of the famed nineteenth century Bibby trooping liners. Streamlined superstructures, one, or at most two, squat funnels and color schemes designed for the "eye appeal" of prospective tourists has made ship-watching more complicated than it used to be, but in most cases the traditional colors and house-flags of the lines remain as the heraldry of the sea.

UMBRIA, 1885

CARONIA, 1904

QUEEN ELIZABETH, 1940

IVERNIA, 1955

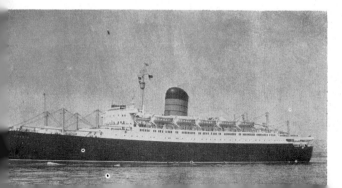

THE CUNARD

The history of the Cunard Line can be read as the history of steam navigation on the North Atlantic. At the dawn of the twentieth century, this great British company had already been in business for six decades. Now, with another sixty years gone by, the story of Cunard is the story of the ocean liner . . . from 200-foot wooden paddle steamer to quadruple-screw, thousand foot super-liner.

The firm was founded by Nova Scotian merchant and shipowner Samuel Cunard who, in 1839 joined forces with Scottish engineer George Napier and British shipowners David MacIver and George Burns, was awarded the Atlantic mail contract by the Admiralty, and ordered four steam packets. The first of them, *Britannia*, sailed from Liverpool on July 4, 1840, making the crossing to Boston in 14 days, eight hours, at an average speed of eight and a half knots. She and her three sister ships registered 1,154 tons and were 207 feet in length. (Any one of them could be stowed comfortably on the foredeck of *Queen Elizabeth*).

By 1900 the weekly Cunard trans-Atlantic service was being maintained by nineteenth century ships far advanced from the wooden paddlers, but equally removed from the great floating cities that were soon to come. There were *Umbria* and *Etruria*, record-breakers of the 1880's, 500-footers of 7,718 tons and speeds of about twenty knots. Their compound engines developed 14,000-horsepower. There were the first twin-screw Cunarders, *Campania* and *Lucania*, over six hundred feet long, of 31,000 horsepower and capable of making better than 23 knots. (It was on *Lucania*, in 1901, that Marconi carried out his practical experiments with wireless telegraphy and in 1903 she published the first ship's newspaper to carry daily wireless news).

The first twentieth century Cunarders, *Caronia* and *Carmania* of 1904, were launched as the biggest ships in the world . . . 675 feet overall and of 19,593 tons. They paved the way for the era of sea giants. *Carmania* was powered by turbines; *Caronia* by orthodox reciprocating engines. Otherwise they were nearly identical. *Carmania* proved faster, smoother and more economical and that was what Cunard had wanted to find out. The incomparable *Lusitania* and *Mauretania*, three years later, were turbine-powered and *their* tonnage was 31,000. Cunard had brought the twentieth century sea giant into being.

Among the well-known lines which have merged with Cunard over the years are Thomson Line (1911), Anchor Line (1912), Commonwealth & Dominion Line (1916), and White Star Line (1934).

SOMALI, 6,708 tons, 1901, at Dartmouth

ORVIETO, 12,133 tons, 1909

STRATHNAVER, 22,547 tons, 1931
ORCADES, 28,164 tons, 1948

P & O ORIENT

For all the soul of our sad East is there
Beneath the house-flag of the P & O.
     . . . Rudyard Kipling

The legendary P & O, "the Cunard of the Eastern Hemisphere," is a company whose history is closely tied to that of the Indian Empire, but the word "Peninsular" in its title refers not to that country, but to the Spanish Peninsula, for when the line had its beginning, in 1836, its two owners, merchant Arthur Anderson and shipbroker Brodie M'Ghie Wilcox, operated their first chartered steamer between London and Spain, as agents for the Peninsular Steam Navigation Company.

In 1837 the line received the Admiralty contract to carry the mail to Lisbon, Cadiz and Gibraltar; three years later, service was extended to Malta and Alexandria and the company name was changed to Peninsular and Oriental. In 1854 the P & O took over the Indian mail service from the ancient East India Company, with additional service to Hong Kong and bimonthly sailings to Singapore and Sydney.

The P & O of the nineteenth century had all the stately dignity and conservatism of the British military officers and civil servants who occupied its liners' first-class quarters on dignified voyages to and from the Far East. The opening of the Suez Canal had brought the compound-engined screw steamer into use by the company and, by the early years of the twentieth century, it had progressed to the use of twin sets of triple-expansion reciprocating engines in its express liners, not primarily for purposes of speed but because twin screws were a comforting safety factor in the vast eastern seas where, as Kipling observed, if you happened to suffer a broken shaft on a single-screw liner you would have ample time to either mend it or eat it. Some of the early twentieth century P & O liners did receive quadruple-expansion engines, but few of them, before the first World War, cruised at much more than 14 knots. It was of the P & O of this period that Kipling wrote, "*Whom neither rivals spur nor contracts speed.*" Even the colors of the ships were conservative; black, white striped hulls, stone-colored upperworks and black funnels.

The post-World War I period, however, brought the steam turbine to the P & O, and the glamorous and colorful *Strath* liners, first of a new breed. The P & O of today has retained the romance of the Far East that has always seemed to surround its ships, but the conservatism has vanished. The great white P & O-Orient Liners are now among the most advanced ships in the world.

FRENCH LINE

The Crimean War of 1854 had demonstrated to the French government the need for an adequate merchant marine; French industry, growing fast in the machine age, was demanding ocean mail service under the French flag. The result was the creation by Imperial decree, on May 2, 1855, of the forerunner of the modern French Line, "Compagnie General Maritime." By 1856 the line was operating a fleet of 27 sailing ships and four screw steamers. The steamers were busy carrying emigrants to the New World; the windjammers freighting cargoes of salted codfish from Newfoundland to the Caribbean. In 1861 the company was authorized to change its name to Compagnie Generale Transatlantique.

The Franco-Prussian War of 1870 was a serious setback to the line, but by 1885 it produced the first of a series of famous ships which brought new standards of luxury to trans-Atlantic travel. The first of these, *La Normandie* was the first liner to be equipped with interior plumbing. Soon the Atlantic voyager would see no more that early-morning ritual of a long line of room stewards emptying chamber pots over the leeward rail. *La Normandie* was followed by *La Gascogne*, *La Bretagne*, *La Champagne* and the great *La Touraine* of 1891, which briefly held the Blue Riband which had for so long been monopolized by the British and German liners.

These ships ushered in twentieth century French line service to the United States, followed in 1906 by the splendid *La Provence*.

These ships, handsome and luxurious as they were, were the French version of the transitional Cunard Liners *Carmania* and *Caronia*; the "sea giants"—600-foot, 15,000-tonners—of 1906 were comparative pigmies after 1907 with the advent of the giant *Lusitania*, *Mauretania* and the even larger British and German liners which followed them. By 1908 the French Line was suffering in the highly competitive struggle for first-class passengers. The answer was the first French turbine liner, the 690-foot four-funnelled *France*, almost twice the tonnage of the former flagship *La Provence* and exceeding that of North German Lloyd's big *Kronprinzessin Cecilie* by 4,000 tons. In service in 1912, she immediately became one of the most popular of the Atlantic liners, being joined in 1921 by the much larger *Paris*, and in 1927 by *Isle de France*.

Until 1962 the crowning achievement of this great line was the splendid Blue Riband winner *Normandie*, an accomplishment which has now been surpassed with the coming of the 1,035-foot *France* (2), newest of the world's great luxury liners.

FRANCE, 23,769 tons, 1912

ISLE DE FRANCE, 43,153 tons, 1927

NORMANDIE, 82,799 tons, 1935

FRANCE, 66,000 tons, 1962

SHAW SAVILL LINE

This line was formed in 1882 by the merging of two old-time sailing ship lines, Shaw, Savill of London, which had already been in the New Zealand trade for thirty years, and Patrick Henderson's Albion Line of Glasgow. As early as 1880, the Albion Line had begun installing refrigerating machinery in its sailing ships for the transportation of frozen meat cargoes from Australia and New Zealand to Great Britain. The combination of frozen cargoes below decks and passengers above was a profitable one which was to continue for a long time. Even the line's 27,000-ton luxury flagship of 1939, *Dominion Monarch,* was equipped to carry a half-million tons of frozen cargo below decks.

The line's first steamer service was carried on by two new steamers of its own, *Arawa* and *Tainui* of 1884, and three former Atlantic liners of White Star, *Ionic, Doric* and *Coptic,* which were refitted with refrigeration plants. The ties between Shaw-Savill and White Star remained close, the color scheme of the Shaw-Savill ships being very similar to that of White Star, except that their black hulls are banded with a white rather than a gold stripe, and their buff funnels are a little darker.

In 1910 the line passed into the control of the White Star group, where it remained until the final dissolution of the latter in 1934. It is now controlled by the Furness-Withy group.

The company's house-flag is a handsome one and is interesting in that it was the original national ensign of New Zealand, adopted by the Maori chiefs and early English traders to protect the status of their ships at sea. The line's pride in its colors is indicated by its tradition of flying the house-flag at sea, a custom most unusual in the British Merchant Navy. The cap badge of the line is this flag, crossed with the "Aberdeen White Star" house-flag of the Aberdeen & Commonwealth Line, taken over by Shaw-Savill in 1933.

The company's newest passenger liners, *Southern Cross* and *Northern Star* depart from the long-time formula of combining ample cargo space with comfortable passenger accommodations. These turbine steamers carry only tourist class passengers in air-conditioned staterooms on their round-the-world voyages to Wellington via Trinidad, Curacao, the Panama Canal, Tahiti, Fiji, Cape Town and Las Palmas.

It is now more than a century since the original Shaw-Savill Company set up business in its modest quarters in Billiter Street, London, but from its grand offices in Leadenhall Street, the line remains a vital link in the chain of British Commonwealth nations.

DORIC, WHITE STAR LINER OF 1883, lower left, was one of three operated by Shaw Savill in early steamship service to New Zealand. **Southern Cross,** lower right, 20,204-ton turbine liner was built in 1955 for around-the-world tour service.

ITALIAN LINE

The present Italian Line was the result of the combination of several shipping companies, the earliest being known as Rubattino, after its founder of a century ago. The merged lines were designated as Navigazinoe Generale Italiana (known familiarly as N.G.I.). In 1876, with the unification of Italy into a single kingdom, the company received its first state subsidy, giving it the funds and prestige needed to enter the competition of first-class Atlantic mail and passenger service.

By 1886 the N. G. I. fleet totalled more than one hundred vessels, the company having absorbed a half dozen more shipping lines. Like those of the other maritime nations, the Italian Line fleet suffered severely in World War I service, losing 27 vessels through enemy action.

Between World Wars the company gained a place among the top contenders in the highly competitive trans-Atlantic luxury trade, ending the twenty-two-year reign of the Cunard speed queen *Mauretania* with the advent of the great *Rex*, which was one of the most beautiful big liners evere built. The Italian Line also developed the use of large motor liners in the first-class passenger trade, the 30,400-ton *Augustus* of 1927 still holding the record as the largest motor passenger liner ever built.

Since the second World War the Italian Line has not re-entered the field of giant super-liners, concentrating on moderate-sized ships of modern and elegant design, including the turbine steamers *Cristoforo Colombo* and *Andrea Doria* and motor liners *Augustus* (2), *Giulio Cesare, Vulcania* and *Saturnia.*

The Italian Liners have long been noted for their handsome, sweeping lines and luxurious interior furnishings. The *Andrea Doria,* victim of a tragic collision with the Swedish-American Liner *Stockholm* in 1956, was considered by many to be the most beautiful of all the modern Atlantic liners.

The *Giulio Cesare,* of 1951 and the *Augustus,* 1952, 27,100-ton sister motor liners and presently the largest diesel-powered passenger carriers in service, are typical of the Italian Line's present-day concept, of moderate size and speed, yet as luxurious as any ships afloat. Their amenities include three swimming pools, one for each class, complete air-conditioning, ship-to-shore telephones and spacious salons staffed by top-flight continental chefs and superbly trained stewards providing the kind of service and cuisine that seems to be unique to the ships of the French and Italian Lines.

ITALIAN LINE COMMODORE

PRESENTLY MASTER of Italian Line's 33,500-ton flagship **Leonardo da Vinci,** Capt. Mario Crepaz, above, is the line's senior officer. Born at Trieste in 1905, Capt. Crepaz began his career as third officer of S.S. **Mario** in 1930, becoming staff captain of M.S. **Vulcania** in 1955 and in 1958 receiving command of M.S. **Antoni-tons,** shortly thereafter, his last command prior to taking over the flagship being the **Leonardo's** sister - ship, the turbine liner **Cristoforo Colombo.**

—ITALIAN LINE PHOTO

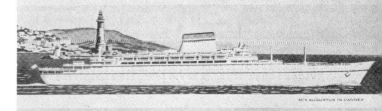

Typical Post-World War I President Liner.

S.S. PRESIDENT HOOVER, 21,936 tons, 1931

S.S. PRESIDENT POLK, 9,260 tons, 1941

S.S. PRESIDENT CLEVELAND, 15,437 tons, 1947

AMERICAN PRESIDENT LINES

The splendid present-day fleet of the American President Lines had its beginnings on the West Coast of the United States with the Dollar Steamship Company which, in turn, began in 1901 with a single diminutive steam schooner, the 200-ton *Newsboy,* operated by lumberman Robert Dollar to haul his timber from the Northwest mills to the California markets.

Today the American President Lines serves more than fifty ports across 70,000 sea miles with 24 ships ranging from freighters to the 23,500-ton flagship *President Cleveland* and her sister-ship, *President Wilson,* both placed in service in 1948 at a cost of $22,000,000 each.

A. P. L. carries on the heritage of the old Pacific Mail Line, which extended its coastal service of gold rush days to operate passenger and mail liners across the Pacific to China, Japan and the Philippines. It was after the turn of the century, with the Pacific Mail being virtually legislated out of business, that Robert Dollar, already nearing sixty years of age, entered the shipping business. He soon expanded his fleet and his service to the Orient and eventually picked up the mail subsidy contracts formerly held by Pacific Mail. Deep-sea shipping superceded logging as Dollar's primary interest and he gradually expanded his freighter service, acquired a major interest in the coastwise Pacific Steamship Company and methodically prepared for entry into the passenger liner field on a major scale.

The surplus World War I 502's and 535's gave him the opportunity he had been looking for. In 1923 he purchased the first fleet of *President* liners from the government. At the age of eighty he inaugurated the famed Dollar Line round-the-world service with the sailing, on January 5, 1924, of the *President Harrison* from San Francisco.

Although the Dollar Line collapsed financially in 1938, the government took over operation temporarily and, since the pioneer sailing of the *President Harrison* four decades ago, *President* liners have been churning a continuous wake around the globe. The company was completely returned to private ownership in 1952 under ownership of American President Lines Associates, Inc., headed by California oil men Ralph K. Davies and Samuel Mosher.

UNION CASTLE LINE

The Union Steam Collier Company was formed in 1853 with the intention of entering the coal-carrying trade. Instead it soon found itself occupied in carrying passengers and mail from Southampton to the Near East and South Africa. The black-hulled, yellow-funnelled Union Line steamers were all given the names of various nationalities . . . *Dane, Celt, Norman, Briton, Saxon,* etc.

Sir Donald Currie's Castle Mail Packet Company, which entered the South African service in 1872, soon became Union's principal rival. The 2,500-ton *Walmer Castle,* which sailed for Table Bay in the early summer of 1872 was the first of the vast fleet of *Castle* liners which was to follow.

At the turn of the century the famous Union Line Cape racer *Scot* and Castle's crack *Dunottar Castle* were fighting it out for the speed championship of the South African run; *Scot's* record of slightly over 14 days for the Southampton-Cape Town run, set in 1893, was only broken by the motor liner *Stirling Castle* in 1936.

The rivalry was expensive, however, and in February, 1900, the Union Line and the Castle Line amalgamated to form the Union-Castle Mail Steamship Co., Ltd., under the management of Donald Currie and Company. The Union fleet at this time consisted of 19 vessels totalling 104,107 tons, the Castle fleet of 20 vessels for a total of 108,886 tons.

The ships of the merged companies kept their original names, but all were painted in the handsome Castle Line colors—lavender-gray hulls, white superstructures and black-topped crimson funnels. As new ships were built they received *Castle* names. On August 10, 1914, the old Union Liner *Norman* and the *Dunvegan Castle* made a place for themselves in history when they landed the first British troops on French soil in World War I.

Long among the largest operators of motor liners, having launched their first one, *Carnarvon Castle* in 1926, the Union-Castle Line has, since the second World War, returned to steam turbine propulsion for its first-class mail liners, including such notable postwar liners as *Edinburgh Castle, Pretoria Castle* and the splendid new flagship of the line, 38,000-ton *Windsor Castle,* built by Cammell Laird and in service in 1960 as the largest British-built ship since *Queen Elizabeth.*

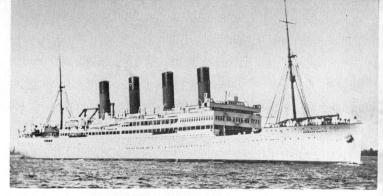

WINDSOR CASTLE, 1922.

CARNARVON CASTLE, 1926.

CAPETOWN CASTLE, 1937.

WINDSOR CASTLE, 1960.

WILHELMINA, 6,974 tons, 1909

MALOLO, 17,231 tons, 1927

MATSONIA, 18,170 tons, 1932

MONTEREY, 14,800 tons, 1957

MATSON
NAVIGATION
COMPANY

Captain William Matson's fleet of San Francisco-Hawaiian sailing ships of the 1880's had, by 1901 become the Matson Navigation Company, steamship operators. The first passenger steamship operated by the company was the little iron-hulled, single screw *Enterprise*, built in 1882. She was followed by the similar iron steamers *Rosecrans*, built in 1883, and *Hilonian* of 1880 vintage.

Regular Matson liner service from the West Coast of the United States to the Islands began with the arrival on the scene of the first of the distinctive funnel-aft steamers built to company specifications, *Lurline* of 1908. The 413-foot *Lurline*, named for Captain Matson's first sailing ship, was followed by the somewhat larger but similar *Wilhelmina* in 1909 and *Matsonia* and *Manoa* in 1913. The last of the pre-World War I Matson Liners, *Maui* of 1917, was similar in appearance to the earlier ships with engines aft, but was powered by twin-screw turbines. Only the blue-topped buff funnels with the blue Matson "M" were similar to the Matson passenger ship colors of today; the dark reddish-brown hulls of the old liners were supplanted by the gleaming white of the present fleet with the arrival on the Pacific in 1927 of the 17,226-ton twin-stacked luxury liner *Malolo* (still in service on the Atlantic as Home Lines' *Queen Frederica*).

In the course of its long and dominant career as an American flag service to Hawaii and across the Pacific, the Matson Navigation Company, like most successful steamship companies, absorbed many competing lines, among them Oceanic and Oriental Line in 1878, California Steamship Company, Los Angeles Steamship Company and the Oceanic Line. (For some time following the latter merger the company was known as Matson-Oceanic Lines).

In addition to its fleet of black-hulled freighters, Matson presently serves America's fiftieth state with the big *Matsonia* and *Lurline*, while its trans-Pacific passenger service is handled by the smaller but equally luxurious *Mariposa* and *Monterey*.

SWEDISH AMERICAN LINE

The traditionally sea-mined Swedes had, by the beginning of the twentieth century, long been anxious to enter ships in the prestige mail and passenger service of the North Atlantic. With the establishment of the Norwegian-American Line in 1913 it became a matter of stubborn Scandinavian pride to do so.

Swedish shipping magnate Dan Brostrom sparked a move to establish a goverment-supported trans-Atlantic steamship line, with a target date of 1915, but the first World War put a halt to his plans. After the war the famous Allan Liner *Virginian* of 1905 vintage, one of the first Atlantic turbine liners, was purchased and completely renovated. She emerged in 1922 as the *Drottningholm* and was successful from the start. Her running-mate was the first *Stockholm*, formerly the 12,850-ton German *Potsdam*, built at Hamburg in 1914. They were followed, in 1925, by the first *Gripsholm*, first of the large post-war Swedish mail and passenger liners and one of the first of the big motor liners, and in 1928 by the first *Kungsholm*, a larger motorship. These two ships proved to be tremendously popular, both in liner and cruise service, and unusually long-lived. The *Kungsholm*, after World War II service as the U. S. Transport *John Ericcson*, is still in service as the Panamanian *Italia*.

The outstanding success of the original motorliners *Kungsholm* and *Gripsholm* set the pattern for Swedish-American ships, its handsome post-World War II liners *Kungsholm*, *Gripsholm* and *Stockholm* all being diesel-driven.

The Swedish-American liners are outstandingly handsome ships, their all-white hulls and superstructures crowned by buff funnels bearing the three golden crowns of Sweden on a blue shield. Like all Scandinavian ships, they are maintained with all the pride and skill of a nation which was producing great seafarers before the dawn of recorded history.

CAPTAIN PER-ERIC SJOLM, above, master of the Swedish-America Line's beautiful motor liner **Kungsholm,** is a "young veteran" of the sea; at 51 he has held master's papers for 26 years. He joined the Swedish-American Line in 1937. In 1954 he took command of the sailing ship **Albatross,** a schooner used to train future officers of the line, sailing the seven seas for two years with his youthful crew of 17 to 21-year-old cadets. Known to passengers and crew alike for his humor and kindliness as well as his splendid seamanship, he has given the **Kungsholm** the reputation of a "happy ship".

CAPTAIN SJOLM'S COMMAND, the famous cruise liner **Kungsholm,** right, is 600 feet long, registers 21,164 tons. She's completely air conditioned with individual control of temperature and air circulation in every stateroom. All cabins are outside, with private bath or shower. Her hull is strengthened for navigating in ice and equipped with stabilizers for smooth sailing. Dutch-built at Flushing, she's driven by twin eight-cylinder Burmeister & Wain diesels.

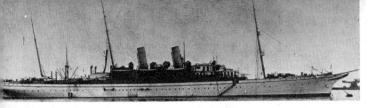

EMPRESS OF JAPAN, 1890

EMPRESS OF ASIA, 1913

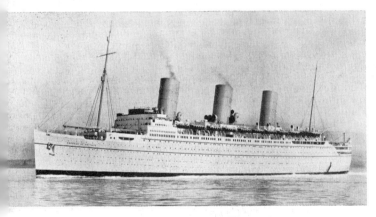

EMPRESS OF BRITAIN, 1930

EMPRESS OF BRITAIN, 1956

CANADIAN PACIFIC STEAMSHIPS

The origin of the Canadian Pacific Railway's famed *Empress* fleets of Atlantic and Pacific liners may be traced back to February 1, 1881, when the railway company was incorporated, designed to link the new western province of British Columbia with a transcontinental railway to the east.

In the course of railway construction, the company ordered three 2,800-ton steamers from Scottish builders to carry material and supplies on the Great Lakes. The *Algoma*, *Alberta* and *Athabaska* inaugurated CPR steamer service in 1884.

With the completion of full transcontinental rail service in 1886, steps were taken to feed Oriental cargo and passengers to the new line. In 1887 several ships were chartered by the railway for trans-Pacific service, including the former Cunarders *Abyssinia*, *Batavia* and the *Parthia* which, as the American *Victoria*, was still in service at the age of 80 as the oldest ship in the American merchant fleet. These ships performed well, but weren't fast enough to meet the specifications of the post office when, in 1889, CPR was awarded an ocean mail contract. This called for 17½-knot ships capable of serving as auxiliary cruisers or troopers in emergency.

The result was the first fleet of white Empresses, the magnificent clipper-stemmed *Empress of China*, *Empress of India* and *Empress of Japan*. All three were delivered in 1891 by the Naval Construction and Armaments Company of Barrow-on-Furness. All exceeded their guaranteed speed of. 18 knots on the measured mile.

In 1903 the Canadian Pacific acquired the 15-ship Beaver Line of the Elder Dempster Company to begin its trans-Atlantic service between Canada and Great Britain. The pioneer Atlantic *Empress* liners, *Empress of Britain* and *Empress of Ireland* were added in 1906, capturing the speed record for the Canadian route from the competing Allan Line turbiners *Virginian* and *Victorian*. The *Empress of Ireland* was victim of a disaster almost as terrible as that of the Titanic when, in 1914, she collided with the Norweigian collier *Storstad* and sank in 15 minutes with a death toll of 1,053.

In 1913 the original Empresses were superceded on the Pacific by the new 13,000-ton *Empress of Russia* and *Empress of Asia*, although the last of them, *Empress of Japan*, remained in service until 1922. Many other great *Empress* liners have served in peace and war on two oceans. The present-day fleet, maintaining the Canadian trans-Atlantic service, consists of the 27,300-ton *Empress of Canada*, launched in 1961, and the 25,000-ton *Empress of Britain* (1956) and *Empress of England* (1957).

UNITED STATES LINES

The United States Lines' history begins in 1921, but generations of sea tradition are behind the great modern ships which carry the blue spread-eagle houseflag across the Atlantic.

In 1930 the United States Lines became a part of the American-owned International Mercantile Marine Company, a combine which included the famous old American Line, whose crack liners of the turn of the century *City of Paris* and *City of New York* proudly flew the eagle houseflag.

After World War I, the American Line was the first to reestablish service to Germany, operating the old liners *Manchuria, Mongolia, Finland, Kroonland* and *Minnekahda* in trans-Atlantic service by late 1919. The *St. Paul* was added to the run in 1922. In 1923 the Atlantic service was virtually abandoned, all but the *Minnekahda* being transferred to the Panama-Pacific Lines, New York to California service, taking the blue spread-eagle houseflag with them. The *Minnekahda* was sold in 1925 and the eagle flag disappeared temporarily from the deep-sea trade routes.

In the meantime, however, the United States shipping Board was operating a European service with eight of the siezed former German liners, including the *George Washington* and *America* (ex-*Amerika*) under the management of the U. S. Mail Steamship Company. In 1921 the ships were placed under the operating managements of the United States Lines, with the huge *Vaterland*, renamed *Leviathan* soon added to the fleet.

When the International Mercantile Marine group purchased the fleet late in 1930 it consisted of the aging and unprofitable *Leviathan, President Roosevelt, President Harding* and a couple of 8,000-ton cargo liners. The *Manhattan* and *Washington* were under construction. They were completed in 1932 and 1933, the largest passenger liners built until that time in the United States and the first big liners to be built in the country since 1905. In 1939 the *America* (2) was launched by Mrs. Franklin D. Roosevelt to take over the record as largest American-built ship, which she held until the commissioning of the super-liner *United States* in 1952.

Today the venerable blue spread-eagle houseflag flies with the Blue Riband of the Atlantic on the great *United States*, flagship of a 50-ship fleet serving most of the world's major ports.

CITY OF NEW YORK, 1889

AMERICA (1), 1905

WASHINGTON, 1933.

AMERICA, 1940.

ESCORTS FOR THE SEA QUEENS: Moore-McCormack's new **Brasil** is ushered past the lower Manhattan skyline by efficient harbor tugs of the Moran fleet, above, while below the 27,300-ton Canadian Pacific flagship **Empress of Canada** is handily swung toward her pier by another pair of Moran's mighty mites.

—FRANK O. BRAYNARD PHOTO

HOLLAND AMERICAN LINE

This great passenger line had its small beginnings in 1871, its thrifty Dutch founders operating it as a private corporation without government subsidy. Its first two small steamers, *Rotterdam* and *Maas* sailed from Rotterdam to New York, as did later Holland-America liners until increasing drafts of the larger liners made it necessary to shift operations to the deep-water port of Amsterdam.

The company's history was one of constant struggles and setbacks (three of its early steamers were lost within a matter of months), but the coming of the twentieth century brought prosperity. New and bigger ships were built and, in 1908, the Neptune Line of Sunderland was purchased from Furness, Withy, who had acquired it two years before; this included the two best of the Neptune steamers, *Ohio* and *Runo*.

During the first World War the neutral Dutch ships reaped a rich harvest as the great liners of the Allied and Central powers turned to war service. Although the line suffered some losses from submarines and mines, it prospered and invested its earnings, after the war, in such spendid big liners as the 25,600-ton *Volendam* of 1923, and the stately *Statendam* of 1929, one of the most beautiful ships ever built on classic ocean liner lines. Although her six steam turbines and twin screws gave her a nice turn of speed, she was an economical ship, in the best tradition of the line's Dutch founders, and was one of the best profit-earners among the big trans-Atlantic liners.

The new pattern was set in 1938 with the launching of the 36,300-ton *Nieuw Amsterdam*, whose raked stem, streamlined superstructure and two short but massive funnels are typical of the later twentieth century liners. In 1939 the old Red Star Line was taken over from the German firm of Arnold Bernstein.

The line's present fleet of Atlantic liners consists of the *Rotterdam*, 38,645 tons, *Nieuw Amsterdam*, 36,982 tons, *Statendam*, 24,292 tons, *Westerdam*, 12,149 tons and *Maasdam*, 15,024 tons.

The reputation of the Holland America Line is among the best, and certainly its history entitles it to its company motto, *Eindelijk wordt een Spruit een Boom* . . . "Finally a sprig becomes a tree".

ROTTERDAM (1) 1872

ROTTERDAM (4) 1908

NIEUW AMSTERDAM, 1938

STATENDAM (4) 1957

ZIM ISRAEL NAVIGATION CO.

ZIM ISRAEL NAVIGATION CO., LTD.

(Zim is derived from the Hebrew "Zi Mischari," which means merchant fleet).

**Zebulon shall dwell at the shores of the sea.
And he shall be a shore for ships.**
. . . Genesis 49:13

As many of the old established trans-Atlantic passenger lines were established to meet the need of the masses of Europe to find a new life in the New World, Zim Lines, which operates two-thirds of Israel's merchant marine, was created with the primary task of carrying emigrants from Europe eastward to the new Promised Land.

The heritage of this new and dynamic force in the maritime world is that of the grim days of **Exodus**, going back to 1945, three years before the State of Israel was given international recognition. (The young Israeli captain of the famous "**Exodus**" of the novel and film is today a master on ships of Zim Israel Navigation Company).

The tremendous pressures of immigration after the second World War (as many as 20,000 arrivals per month during 1948-49) forced the company to seek tonnage on the second-hand ship market. The first ship to fly the Star of David was the little **Kedah** of 2,499 tons, built by Vickers in 1927 for the Singapore-Malay Straits service of the Straits Steamship Co. of Singapore, which, renamed slightly (**Kedmah**), ran the Marseilles, Naples, Haifa run for two years before Israel gained independence.

Even then it was the goal of Zim Israel to develop competitive service on the Mediterranean and Atlantic routes. By 1950, "making do" with its slow and ancient ships, it had passenger and cargo services on the Mediterranean, a cargo line to Western Europe, the beginnings of service to West Africa, and was a partner in the Israel America Line, which sent the first Israeli Flag ships to the United States and Canada.

The Bonn-Israel reparations pact of 1952 provided Israel with 34 new ships built in West German yards. Today Zim Israel operates 42 modern cargo ships and five sleek passenger liners, with their trans-Atlantic liners averaging 89% of capacity in 1962, probably the highest of any Atlantic passenger ships.

Soon the twenty million dollar, 23,000-ton **Shalom** will join the fleet, climaxing one of the most dramatic stories of courage and determination in the world's maritime history.

GALILAH, 3,899 tons, 1913, was once Hudson Day Liner **Dewitt Clinton.**

JERUSALEM, 11,015 tons, 1913, was Norwegian **Bergensfjord;** later Home Line's **Argentina.**

ZION, 9,855 tons, 1956, is fine, modern luxury liner on New York-Haifa service.

M. S. MOLEDET, 1961, is all-tourist liner in service between Israel and Europe.

MOORE-McCORMACK LINES

MOORE-McCORMACK LINE, one of America's largest steamship enterprises, celebrated in 1963 the 50th anniversary of the voyage which launched the company's growth from a single-ship operation into a four-continent American Flag shipping service. It was in July of 1913 that the freighter **Montara,** under charter to the then unknown firm of Moore & McCormack, reached Rio de Janeiro on the first call by a United States merchant ship to that port in 26 years.

The reception given the new service by Brazilian and American shippers convinced the partners that an American Flag service on this route was needed. With the backing of J. P. Morgan, the American Republic Lines was developed, with passenger service introduced in 1915. Moore-McCormack also entered the Atlantic trade, with services to Scandinavia, Poland and Russia.

In 1938 Moore-McCormack responded to President Roosevelt's call for regular American Flag liner service to South American east coast ports with its famous Good Neighbor service via the rebuilt liners **Argentina, Brazil** and **Uruguay.** During World War II the line operated 707 ships for the United States government. During the Korean War it was the Moore-McCormack-operated freighter **Meredith Victory** that astounded the world by rescuing in **one voyage** 14,000 refugees from the advancing North Koreans.

The new and ultra-modern **Argentina** (above) and **Brasil** replaced the old **Argentina, Brasil** and **Uruguay** in 1958. These 22,770-ton twins, 617 feet in length, were built by Ingalls Shipbuilding Corporation, Pascagoula, Mississippi, are driven at 23-knot speeds by 17,500-horsepower steam turbines and twin screws. Handsomely decorated and completely air-conditioned, each ship has two swimming pools, theater, deck cafe, library, gift shop and many other facilities for luxurious one-class cruising.

Completing his final voyage before retirement, Moore-McCormack Commodore Thomas N. Simmons, center right, stepped ashore from the new **Argentina** in April, 1963. His half-century at sea began in sail as a deck boy. He took command of the old **Argentina** when she went into service in 1938; stayed with her throughout her career, including World War II trooping service.

—MOORE-McCORMACK LINES PHOTOS

BELOW: ARGENTINA (1), 1929

BRASIL

ITALIA

HOMERIC

QUEEN FREDERICA

HOME LINES

The Home Lines was founded in 1946, soon after the cessation of the hostilities of World War II, by the late Eugen (OK) Eugenides, who was well known and respected in international circles. Mr. Eugenides, a man of great ambition and ingenuity, a tremendous capacity for work, broad business experience, keen foresight and an ability for far-reaching, detailed planning, foresaw a great need for passenger ship tonnage during the reconstruction period following World War II and he formed Home Lines to participate in this trade.

Home Lines first step was the acquisition of the liner *Argentina* and, in January of 1947, the establishment of the first post-war regular passenger service between Italy and Argentina, Brazil and Uruguay. Fifteen months later, the *Brasil* was purchased and put into operation on this service; and in July of 1948 a third vessel, the *Italia*, further augmented this run.

The next progression brought Home Lines into the New York-Mediterranean passenger trade with a regular service by the *Atlantic* and the *Italia*, which had been withdrawn from a then fading trade between Italy and South America. Two years later, as that continent's economic difficulties mounted, the Home Lines suspended its service and later sold the *Argentina* and *Brasil* to make room for improved tonnage.

In 1954, at the request of the Greek Government, Home Lines formed a subsidiary company, the National Hellenic American Line, and placed the *Atlantic* under the Greek flag, with her named changed to *Queen Frederica* in honor of the reigning Queen of Greece. The *Queen Frederica* still operates between New York and Spain, Gibraltar, Italy and Greece. With some time off for winter cruises to the Caribbean area.

Early in 1961, after several years of intensive planning, Home Lines contracted for the 34,000-ton super-liner *Oceanic*. The Cantieri Reuniti dell'Adriatico shipyard at Monfalcone, Italy, will deliver this great new liner during the first part of 1964 as the company's new flagship. Her addition will raise the fleet of Home Lines to four liners—*Homeric, Italia, Queen Frederica* and the new *Oceanic*.

AMERICAN EXPORT LINES

This was another of the American shipping companies born of the need of the Shipping Board to find use for its tremendous fleet of World War I-built ships. As the Export Steamship Corporation, it began service in 1919 to Mediterranian and Near East ports with a fleet of the standardized "Hog Islanders", the Liberty ships of World War I.

In 1930-31 it acquired its first cargo-passenger liners, the original "Four Aces", *Excalibur*, *Excambion*, *Exeter* and *Exochorda*. By 1934 it had also accumulated debts of eight million dollars; the entire fleet—the 20 old Hog Islanders and the "Four Aces"—was purchased for a million and a half dollars by a small syndicate backed by the Lehman interests.

Under the new management the company began to operate in the black and by 1939, with European competition almost wiped out by the gathering clouds of war, it began earning phenomenal profits. In 1939 the line extended service to India by purchase of the four motorship fleet of the American Pioneer Line, and pioneered in trans-Atlantic air transportation with the operation of a fleet of flying boats from New York to Marseilles via the Azores. (The company is still a major stockholder in American Overseas Airways).

During the war American Export Lines operated 80 ships in addition to its own vessels, losing seven of its Hog Islanders, one of its later *Export* class freighters and three of the original "Four Aces", two in the invasion of North Africa and one at Guadalcanal. (The fourth Ace, *Exochorda*, became the Turkish State Maritime S. S. *Tarus* in 1951.

After the war the line converted four former attack transports, gave them the names of the old "Four Aces" and resumed the express passenger and freight service from New York to Alexandria. For a time the line operated the *La Guardia* (now the American President Lines' *President Roosevelt*) between New York and Israeli via Gibralter, Greece and Italy.

On February 10, 1951, the line's 26,000-ton luxury liner *Independence* began her maiden voyage from New York to Genoa. She was followed, on June 21, by her sister-ship, *Constitution*. Built by Bethlehem Steel's Quincy, Massachusetts yard, these 26-knot turbine liners were designed to provide American luxury living standards at sea as well as incorporating the ultimate in safety factors.

LaGUARDIA, 17,951 tons, 1944

INDEPENDENCE, CONSTITUTION, 23,719 tons, 1950, 1951.

ATLANTIC, 18,100 tons, 1960

101

Third Class Rates

Great Britain, Ireland & The Continent

White Star Line

CONSOLIDATED TICKET OFFICE
J. C. PERCIVAL, Agent
224 State Ave. - Olympia

H-5380   Printed in U. S. A.

WHITE STAR LINE

During the Australian gold rush days of the early 1850's a line of clipper ships was established for Liverpool to Australia service. Their houseflag displayed a large five-pointed star and the line was known popularly as the White Star Line.

When Thomas Ismay, director of the National Line, took over as managing owner of the White Star in 1867 the wooden clippers were superceded by iron steamers and, in 1869 he founded the Oceanic Steam Navigation Company, introducing the White Star flag to the Atlantic. Harland & Wolff of Belfast constructed a number of fine liners for the new service, so far advanced over the existing Western Ocean ships that they established firmly the reputations of both the builders and the owners. The first of these, the *Oceanic,* was the first Atlantic liner to shift passenger accommodations from aft, an uncomfortable holdover from sailing ship days, to amidships cabins. The established companies quickly followed suit in the design of their ships, and for the first time, marine architects were required to give thought to means of adequate ventilation. The *Oceanic* ended the ancient era of the stench of bilgewater and unwashed humanity at sea.

In 1889 the company again made maritime history with the construction of the first *Majestic* and the *Teutonic* as armed merchant cruisers built to Admiralty specifications, and in 1899 the second *Oceanic* was placed in service, the first ship in the world to exceed in size Brunel's *Great Eastern* of 1860.

British pride was badly bruised when the American-owned International Mercantile Marine trust gained control of the White Star in 1902. Following large scale wartime service from 1914 to 1918, which saw the loss of the line's *Britannic* which, at 47,000 tons was the largest British-built liner of those days, the White Star reverted to British ownership in 1926. At this time the White Star owned a controlling interest in Shaw Savill & Albion, Aberdeen Line and Aberdeen & Commonwealth Line.

In 1934 the Atlantic services of White Star were merged with those of Cunard, including such world record-holding White Star liners as *Majestic* (largest ship), *Olympic* (largest British-built ship), *Homeric* (largest twin-screw ship) and *Georgic* (largest British motorship and largest cabin liner). As long as any of the original White Star Liners remained in service they retained their traditional White Star color scheme and the White Star houseflag was flown with the golden lion of Cunard on all the ships of the merged fleets. The last of them, M. S. *Britannic* has now gone out of service and the White Star tradition is gone from the North Atlantic.

SCANDINAVIAN AMERICAN LINE

The glamor of the tall-stacked ocean liner of the 1920's was first revealed to the writer by the gift of a huge painting of the Scandinavian-American Line flagship *Frederick VIII* reproduced, frame and all, on a sheet of tin. It was obtained as a small boy, after a determined campaign of many months duration, from J. C. Percival, principal steamship agent of my home town, Olympia, Washington. Mr. Percival had operated his dock and ticket office since the early 1880's and had similar huge and brilliantly-colored portraits of almost every ocean liner since the *Umbria*. He was reluctant to part with any of them and I only got the *Frederick VIII* because the Scandinavian-American people had a particularly generous publicity department and Mr. Percival had at least a dozen similar tin masterpieces stacked in his back room.

The *Frederick VIII* was really a modest vessel, an 11,850-ton twin-screw steamer driven by a pair of reciprocating engines and with an overall length of just over 523 feet, built at Stettin, Germany in 1913. But in the painting she loomed tall as the clouds, her pair of mighty red-banded black funnels belched awesome clouds of smoke, and the bone in her teeth resembled a minor tidal wave.

By 1927 the line boasted a fleet of 115 steamers and 10 motorships, but after the second World War it did not return to the Atlantic passenger run. Recently I saw a big tin lithograph of the *Frederick VIII* hanging behind the desk of a skid road hotel in Seattle, a duplicate of my boyhood prize.

The old liner, long vanished from the sea, still belched smoke from her tall red and black funnels and plowed her painted bow wave through fly-specked seas. The Scandinavian-American Liners no longer sail "sharp on time" from their pier at the foot of 17th Street Hoboken for Copenhagen, Christiania, Christiansand, Bergen and Frederikshavn, but to me at least the *Frederick VIII* is not forgotten.

MAURETANIA (1) (above)
BELOW: OLYMPIC, TITANIC, AQUITANIA

PARCEL DELIVERY BY AEROPLANE TO SHIP AT SEA

SOPWITH

MR. SOPWITH FLYING OVER THE OLYMPIC AS SHE LEAVES PORT.

The aeroplane has at last been put to commercial use in a most remarkable manner. When W. A. Burpee, the millionnaire seedman of Philadelphia, left New York on the Olympic he suddenly remembered that he had forgotten several important articles of wearing apparel. The liner had already left its pier. The Olympic is equipped with wireless telegraph, as is also a well known New York department store, a member of which was sailing on the same vessel. To him Mr. Burpee made known his predicament.

In a jiffy the order was sent by wireless, accompanied by a request that the stuff be delivered on the Olympic even though an aeroplane had to be employed. Five minutes after the wireless was received a contract was closed with Aviator Sopwith, who was tuning up his machine on Long Island. Three-quarters of an hour later the aeroplane skimmed gracefully over the deck of the Olympic and dropped the package for Mr. Burpee, who was almost overcome with astonishment.

AIR MAIL PIONEER Sopwith made aviaton history in 1911 along with the first air mail delivery to a ship at sea, R.M.S. **Olympic** of the White Star Line.

Chapter Five
BALLIN'S BIG THREE

. . . And Other Ocean Liner Tales

Behold now Behemoth . . .
His bones are as strong pieces of brass;
His bones are like bars of iron.
—Job XI, 15-24

The term "super-liner" is frowned upon by most purists in the realm of maritime nomenclature on the grounds that it was coined by the press agent rather than the seaman or engineer. It seems to be a useful term, however, to describe the sea giants that have gone far beyond the standard definition of a "first-class liner". A first-class liner is generally considered to be a passenger vessel of 20,000 or more gross tons and capable of a speed of 20 knots or better. But what of the twentieth century liners of two, three or four times that tonnage and capable of much higher speed?

Even among those who accept the term, there is considerable disagreement as to just what ship ushered in the era of the super-liner. Although the term has come into popular use only in recent years it might well have been applied to those three gigantic ships of half a century ago, *Imperator*, *Vaterland* and *Bismark*.

The brain children of the Hamburg American Line's managing director, Albert Ballin, these pre-World War I super-liners were built in German yards, designed to eclipse in size and splendor anything then afloat . . . especially anything owned by the British Cunard Line and the rival German company, North German Lloyd.

Hamburg American had been doing well for a long time with ships of moderate size and speed which hauled huge steerage cargoes of emigrants across the Atlantic, but its efforts to break into the select company of the highest-speed sea giants had not been spectacularly successful. The lean four-stacker *Deutschland*, built to challenge the North German Lloyd greyhounds had picked up North Atlantic speed trophy for a while, but she was an inconsistent performer and some of her passages were as remarkably slow as others were fast. She was soon withdrawn from the competition of the North Atlantic run and placed in leisurely cruise service.

Although the new liners were designed to carry the usual horde of steerage passengers below decks, their first-class facilities were the most lavish ever seen; veritable floating museums of ponderous Teutonic carving in dark woods, oil paintings, marble, stained

glass, heroic statues, gilt-framed mirrors and curving mahogany stairways.

Imperator, built by Vulcan at Hamburg, was the first of the trio to be launched—in the spring of 1912. She made here maiden voyage to New York the following summer, receiving the traditional waterfront welcome accorded sea queens making their debut. She was certainly impressive and undoubtedly the biggest thing afloat. Her gross tonnage of 52,226 was nearly equal to that of the super-liner *United States* of today. She measured over 900 feet and she could carry 4,235 passengers, which is more than the combined passenger and crew capacity of today's largest liner.

Still, *Imperator* had her share of critics, who compared her square and ponderous bulk unfavorably with the dainty grace of *Lusitania* and *Mauretania*. It was also pointed out that Ballin's architects had gone to obvious extremes to increase her overall length. The tremendous overhang of her stern might be accepted, but not the huge, gilt-encrusted eagle figurehead perched on a golden globe at the liner's prow. This was certainly a heavy-handed artifice to increase her length for the benefit of the advertising department. And people who were disturbed at growing signs of German imperialism shuddered at the motto carved on the eagle's perch . . . *My Field is the World.*

After a voyage or two *Imperator* butted into a particularly heavy sea and the controversial figurehead was seen no more. She also lost a great deal of her massive carved furniture, a number of tremendous marble bathtubs from her luxury suites, the marble-columned continental grill from her promenade deck and nine feet of the top of each of three great funnels, all removed to reduce her topheaviness and improve her stability. In her early North Atlantic voyage she listed horribly whenever her helm was shifted, frightening not only her passengers, but her crew as well. The removal of tons of ponderous bric-a-brac from topside helped, but it was eventually necessary to pour some two thousand tons of concrete in her bottom to keep her right side up.

About a year after the *Imperator* came *Vaterland*, at 54,282 tons and 950-foot overall length the new title-holder of world's largest ship. Ballin's designers had learned a good deal from the troubles of *Imperator* and also from the loss of the *Titanic*, which had occurred in the interim between the two German ships. *Vaterland* looked very much like *Imperator*, but was a half-knot faster, enjoyed excellent stability in heavy seas and, unlike the *Titanic*, had water-tight subdivisions that would really work in an emergency.

World War I broke out with the third of the Ballin trio, *Bismark*, still unfinished at the fitting-out dock in Hamburg. The *Imperator* was also in Hamburg and remained there safely with the unfinished *Bismark* for the duration.

Vaterland, having just reached New York on her third voyage, was laid up there until the United States entered the war in 1917. Then her German crew destroyed her blueprints, dismantled her engines and set about thoroughly mixing up her miles of fuel, water and steam lines. They hooked up pipes and lines to the wrong outlets and then painted out the distinguishing colors which would give a clue to the complex network.

The American boarding party which took over was nonplussed to find the toilets flushing live steam and the showers spraying them with fuel oil or bilge water.

To the annoyance of the Germans, the vast confusion was sorted out in a couple of months and *Vaterland*, renamed *Leviathan*, served as an American transport throughout the war. Capable of carrying

LAND AND SEA GIANTS

LEVIATHAN, BUILT IN GERMANY as the **Vaterland,** was America's first super-liner, but even many patriotic Americans shunned her. She sailed in prohibition days and was the only big liner that served only soft drinks and "near beer" in her luxurious bars.

—UNITED STATES LINES PHOTO

ALBERT BALLIN'S Bismark, under American colors as **Leviathan,** saw a brief period of successful operation as a troop transport during World War I. She's pictured here in wartime gray, as she appeared in 1918.

—U. S. SHIPPING BOARD PHOTO

10,000 troops each voyage, she was a huge success, which she certainly was not during her subsequent career under the American flag.

After the war Great Britain had pressing need for liners to replace its tremendous war losses, which had included Cunard's *Lusitania* and White Star's 48,000-ton flagship *Britannic,* which had been torpedoed before making a single peacetime voyage. The United States had been chronically short of first-class ocean liners since long before the turn of the century.

Germany was ordered to complete the *Bismark* and turn her over, along with *Imperator* and *Leviathan,* as part of her war reparations. The Americans, having operated *Imperator* briefly as a troopship after the armistice, would have none of her. The British Cunard and White Star Lines jointly took over *Imperator* and *Bismark,* Cunard operating the *Imperator* as the *Berengaria* and White Star the *Bismark* under the new name of *Majestic. Leviathan* remained under the American colors, operated first by the soon bankrupt United States Mail Line, then by the government-owned United States Lines and, briefly, by the same company under the private ownership of the International Mercantile Marine group.

EUROPE EUROPE

PROPOSED
SAILINGS
AND
RATES
FOR PASSAGE

AMERICAN LINE
ATLANTIC TRANSPORT LINE
LEYLAND LINE
RED STAR LINE
WHITE STAR LINE
WHITE STAR CANADIAN

PANAMA PACIFIC LINE

PROPOSED
SAILINGS
AND
RATES
FOR PASSAGE

AMERICAN LINE
ATLANTIC TRANSPORT LINE
LEYLAND LINE
RED STAR LINE
WHITE STAR LINE
WHITE STAR CANADIAN

PANAMA PACIFIC LINE

CONSOLIDATED TICKET OFFICE
J. C. PERCIVAL, Agent
224 State Ave. - Olympia
Percival's Dock

CONSOLIDATED TICKET OFFICE
J. C. PERCIVAL, Agent
224 State Ave. - Olympia
Percival's Dock

MAJESTIC, FORMERLY THE GERMAN LINER Bismarck, was the pride of the White Star and affiliated lines when this brochure was printed a generation ago. White Star and the United States Lines carried on a running quarrel for years over whether the **Majestic** or the American **Leviathan** was the largest ship in the world.

BALLIN'S IMPERATOR, once the pride of the German merchant fleet, ended her carrer as **Berengaria** of the Cunard Line.

Leviathan was never able to earn her keep, although she was refitted at Newport News after the war at almost twice the cost of her original construction and emerged as probably the soundest and certainly the fastest of the Ballin trio. The Volstead Act had made her a "dry" ship, causing convivial travelers to shun her like a plague-ship. Unlike *Berengaria*, with her consorts *Mauretania* and *Aquitania*, and *Majestic*, running with the *Titanic's* giant sister *Olympic* and the

big former German liner *Homeric*, the *Leviathan* had to run independently. There were no other American liners in her class. The depression finished off the *Leviathan*. She made her last regular trans-Atlantic voyages in 1932, made a few in 1934, and then was laid up permanently. On a gloomy winter day in 1937 America's first super-liner steamed in shabby solitude on her last voyage, to the Rosyth scrapyards in Scotland. Her passing was unmourned except by a hand-

full of waterfront setimentalists.

The depression brought evil days to *Berengaria* too. Cunard pulled her off the trans-Atlantic run and dispatched her on a series of cut-rate cruises to Bermuda and the West Indies. Her stewards, used to the luxury days when champagne and twenty dollar bills flowed like water, observed their ship's new clientel sipping beer and keeping slim wallets in theadbare pockets and rechristened the aging sea queen *Bargain-area!* For the old *Imperator* this was a worse humiliation than the scrapyard, but her days were numbered in any event. After a series of stubborn between-bulkhead fires which gave warning of faulty wiring, she too went to the scrappers in 1938.

The *Majestic*, transferred with the rest of the White Star fleet to Cunard ownership in 1934, ran briefly with the *Berengaria;* was laid up in 1936 with the completion of *Queen Mary.* Scheduled for the scrapyard, she was reprieved when the Admiralty purchased her for a cadet training ship, but her lease on life was brief. A fire on board made it necessary to scuttle her in the Firth of Forth, where she lay until 1943, when her German steel went to feed the munitions factories of Britain.

It is ironic that these three great ships, built as the living symbols of German pride, spent almost all their lives in the service of Germany's enemies, even the bones of the behemoths going, at last, to make weapons of war to blast the Third Reich of the Nazis.

As for the man who conceived them, the brilliant German Jew, Albert Ballin, he died a few years after they were built. Fiercely proud of the Fatherland, Ballin committed suicide as Germany's hour of defeat drew near.

THE 33,000-TON LUXURY "hotel ship" **Transvaal Castle,** next page, is the newest liner to join the Union-Castle Company's Mail Service to South Africa. This splendid ship sailed on her maiden voyage January 18, 1962.
—RALSTON PHOTO BY UNION-CASTLE LINE

WHITE STAR LINE'S
BIG TWO

Before the beginning of the 1890's the Cunard Line had regained the Atlantic speed record with its powerful single-screw liners *Umbria* and *Etruria*. Donald Ismay's rival British company, the White Star Line, hadn't produced a record-breaker since the old *Britannic* and *Georgic* of 1875. The canny Ismay introduced legislation in Parliament providing for government subsidized construction of large, fast liners suitable for wartime use as armed merchant cruisers, a system still in use among most major maritime nations.

The new law was duly passed and Ismay at once produced completed drawings for a pair of fine new ships which met the specifications perfectly. The keels for the new twin-screw White Star Liners *Majestic* and *Teutonic* were laid down early in 1887. The Inman Line rushed to take advantage of the windfall, too, with plans for its clipper-bowed *City of Paris* and *City of New York*. The era of the twin-screw passenger liners came in with a rush, and the rivalry of the four subsidized ocean racers was to continue well into the twentieth century.

Like all White Star ships, *Majestic* and *Teutonic* were long and slim . . . 582 feet overall with a 57-foot, eight-inch beam (Thirty-eight feet longer, but five and a half feet narrower than the Inman *City* liners). They were the longest ships in the world at the time of their construction, but the added beam of the Inman Liners made them nearly a thousand tons larger in measurement tonnage.

The new White Star sisters were slim and graceful in appearance, yet gave the impression of speed and power. Like the Inman twin-screw ships, these carried no sails, which was an innovation in the ocean steamships of the day and dramatic proof of the reliability of their dual propulsion system. Their big triple-expansion engines, fed by a battery of 16 coal-fired boilers, could work up to almost 20,000 horsepower and well over 20 knots.

Inman's *City of Paris* beat the White Star twins into service and in August of 1889 managed to beat the record of the Cunard Liner *Etruria*, further making history by crossing the Atlantic in under five days. The *City of New York* soon joined her in dramatic transoceanic races with *Majestic* and *Teutonic*. Slow starters, the White Star liners gradually built up to full speed and in 1891 *Teutonic* took both eastward and westward crossings to win the Blue Riband.

All four were beaten two years later by Cunard's new *Campania* and it was the end of White Star's rivalry for the speed trophy. Afterward the line concentrated on large, luxurious ships of moderate speed, culminating in the giant twins *Olympic* and *Titanic* of 1912.

FOLLOWING PAGES: COMPLEX ENGINE ROOM OF S.S. AMERICA houses the six geared turbines which drive the 26,454-ton liner across the Atlantic at 24 knots.

—UNITED STATES LINES PHOTO

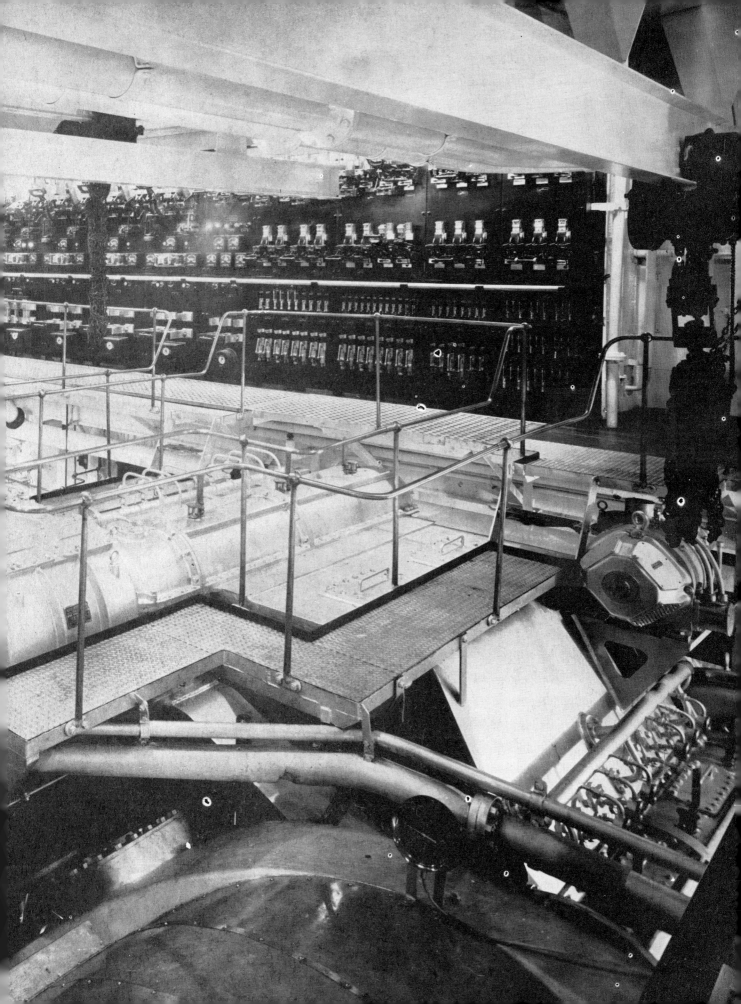

S.S. OHIO in the ice, Alaska.

The Old Ohio . . .

IN DISTANT SEAS

When the old Atlantic liner *Ohio* met her end in Alaskan waters on the morning of November 20, 1909 she terminated a long career abruptly, going down in less than thirty minutes. Of the 213 souls aboard, most were asleep, but skill and seamanship limited the loss of passengers' lives to two.

Built by the Cramp yard at Philadelphia, the *Ohio* was one of the four iron-hulled steamers that temporarily put the American flag back on the North Atlantic where it had been missing since before the Civil War. All four were destined to survive long beyond the two score years and five normally allotted as the economic life span of a passenger liner, and all were to meet their end in far corners of the world, far removed from each other and from the seas they had been designed to steam.

Like her sisters, *Illinois, Indiana* and *Pennsylvania, Ohio* was a single-screw, single-stack craft with a length of 243 feet and a gross tonnage of 3,488. No flyers, they were considered doing well when they were able to maintain an average sea speed of 13 knots during a crossing, but they were reasonably comfortable and were considered by seamen and seasoned travelers to be lucky ships.

They were built for the Inman Line, later the American Line, owned by Philadelphians and backed by the Pennsylvania Railway. The Inman Line had been in the trans-Atlantic trade since early in the 1850's, but with its ships flying the British flag. This was caused by the fact that although United States law forbids the enrollment of foreign-built ships under the American flag there were, at that time, no American shipyards capable of building trans-Atlantic passenger liners. The four Philadelphia-built ships became the first Inman Liners to fly the American flag.

Operating out of Philadelphia to Queenstown and Liverpool, they carried thousands of Irish immigrants west to help maintain the Pennsylvania's rail revenues, but most travelers to Europe were in the habit of departing from New York and the steamers relied heavily on Pennsy Line freight to pay their way on the eastward crossings.

When the Inman twin-screw flyers *City of New York* and *City of Paris* were transferred to American registry by special act of congress, the four plodding sisters were put out of work and lay idle for some time,

being too large for coastwise routes and too slow for the trans-Atlantic run. With the Alaska gold rush in 1897 they were transferred to Seattle for the Yukon Service of the International Mercantile Marine-backed Empire Line.

Then the Spanish-American War of 1898 gave them a new lease on life. The Navy took over *Indiana* and *Illinois*, the latter remaining at Guam as a store ship for the next 28 years. *Pennsylvania* and *Ohio* went trooping for the Army to the Philippines, after which the *Pennsylvania* entered upon a somewhat disreputable career under South American ownership and was eventually destroyed by fire in Iquique Bay, Chile in 1918.

The *Ohio*, along with the old Cunarder *Parthia*, renamed *Victoria* and awarded American citizenship as a result of the Spanish War service, ended up in the service of the Alaska Steamship Company of Seattle. This line's service to Nome favored iron ships which could buck Arctic ice flows that would crush a steel-hulled vessel.

The *Ohio* had been dependably serving the Far North for some years when bad luck finally caught up with her. At one o'clock of that Friday morning in 1909 she was threading her way up the Inside Passage toward Ketchikan. It was a dirty night, with vicious seas kicking up as the *Ohio* entered Findlay Channel, a narrow gut between 3,000-foot-high hills. The charts said the water was deep right inshore, but the Alaska pilot and the *Ohio's* master were on the bridge and on their toes, for the hydrographic surveys of Alaskan waters were sketchy in those days and the Alaska Liners frequently found uncharted rocks the surveyors had missed. The *Ohio* found one of them that night and, steaming at ten knots, she ripped her bottom open for a hundred feet. She was backed off and headed for the beach, but sank in still relatively deep water, with only the tops of her masts and a few feet of her tall funnel above the surface.

The purser, who had returned to the ship for the contents of the safe, was drowned, as was the radio operator, who stayed with his set. A quartermaster drowned with the drunken soldier he was trying to rescue, and a steerage passenger was struck and killed when a lifeboat capsized on the beach.

The loss of only five lives among 213 in a sudden sinking on a wild night in treacherous Alaskan waters added up to an achievement that deserves to take its place in the annals of discipline and good seamanship.

As for the old *Ohio*, whose bones still rust along the Inside Passage of Alaska, she had written more than her share of American ocean liner history in two oceans and two centuries.

YUKON GOLDRUSHERS responded in droves to the advertisement above, for compared to many of the old bay and river steamboats and superannuated hulks used to carry passengers to the gold fields in 1897-98, the **Ohio** and her sister liners were floating palaces.

THE BONES OF THE OLD OHIO bleached for years along the inside passage.

VICTORIA AS SHE LOOKED IN 1870 when she was the Cunard Line's first **Parthia**, above. Lower left, **Victoria's** engine room. Opposite Page: **Victoria** in the ice, Nome Roadstead. Her heavy iron hull gave her a big advantage in bucking her way through Arctic ice.

OLD VIC

When the Cunard Line's first *Parthia* left the building ways of W. Denny & Bros. at Dumbarton, Scotland back in 1870 her arrival caused scarcely a ripple in the maritime world. Her owners had not produced an Atlantic record-holder since the advent of *Russia* three years earlier and were entering upon that long period of eclipse during which no Cunard Liners held the Blue Riband until the coming of *Etruria* in 1885.

Parthia was not built for Cunard's primary service, but for the low-cost emigrant trade between Ireland and the United States. She had no fancy frills and her compound engine developed only 1,800-horsepower, about half that of the average first-class trans-Atlantic liner of her day. During her 15 years of Cunard service on the Atlantic her three bark-rigged masts often carried a full press of canvas, for she had a specially designed propeller which could be disconnected and feathered when the wind was favorable. Having no tight schedule to keep, she often saved

coal in this manner, no doubt to the delight of Cunard's shareholders.

Parthia went to war for the first time in 1881, as a British trooper in the Egyptian campaign. Turned back to Cunard, she was "traded in" in 1885 to builder John Elder as part payment on the new *Etruria* and *Umbria*. After receiving a more powerful triple-expansion engine, she entered the long-haul trade between England, Australia, the Hebredes and South America. After that she became one of the pioneer Canadian Pacific trans-Pacific fleet of 1887, before the coming of the original "White Empresses" in 1891. Then she went back to England for another overhaul, receiving also her new name, *Victoria*. She was then 22 years old and had reached the end of an average passenger ship's life expectancy, but *Victoria* was just getting started. Returning to the Pacific, she spent some years on the Tacoma-Oriental run under management of Dodwell and Company, taking time off for service as a U. S. Army transport during the Spanish American war, after which she was granted American registry.

In 1903 she was taken over for the Alaska trade by the Northwestern Steamship Company, but like an old war-horse, she sniffed the gunpowder of the Russo-Japanese war and made a blockade-running expedition with supplies for the Russians at Vladivostok. Returning to the Seattle-Alaska run, she hoisted the Black Ball houseflag of the Alaska Steamship Company when that line absorbed the Northwestern in 1908.

A plodder on the Atlantic, she became noted as a racer on the Alaska run, frequently challenging and beating the somewhat less elderly *Ohio*. She made her last passenger run in 1937, but put on war **paint**

once again for service through World War II in Alaskan waters.

By 1952 she was, at the age of 82, the grand old lady of America's merchant fleet; the oldest deep-sea ship in service. Her hull of Swedish wrought-iron was still sound, her engine, built by John Elder in 1885 still smooth and powerful, but her slim lines and narrow hatches made her impractical for modern cargo-handling methods. She became a barge, back under British registry in the fleet of Straits Towing Company of Victoria.

Two years later, as the Japanese *Straits Maru*, the slim iron hull was loaded with scrap metal and towed to Japan for final dismantling.

A little old lady of humble origins had ended a long and proud career.

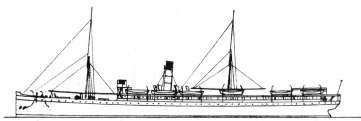

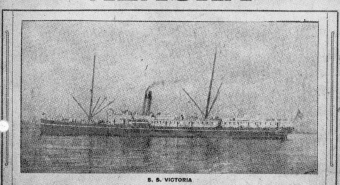

DRAMATIC PROGRESS of a few years by Zim Israel Navigation Company is pictured here. Early emigrant carrier **Negbah,** above, was built in Holland in 1915 as S.S. **Ecuador,** was later Libby, McNeil Company's **David W. Branch.**

S.S. JERUSALEM, center, built in 1957 to replace the original **Jerusalem** of 1913 vintage, plies the Mediterranean in the summer, makes two New York-Haifa voyages a year, and spends the winter on Caribbean cruises out of New York and Miami.

S.S. SHALOM (Peace), below, now under construction at the famed Penhoet yard in St. Nazaire, was launched late in 1962, is expected in service early in 1964. A 23,000-ton luxury liner of the most advanced design, complete with air-conditioning, closed-circuit TV, "sauna" baths, three swimming pools and night club, she will make seven or eight New York-Haifa sailings yearly and operate in cruise service during the off season.

—ZIM ISRAEL NAVIGATION CO. PHOTOS

INTERIORS: THE ORNATE AND CARVEN splendor of the first class Dining Salon on P & O's **Maloja** of 1911, above, is in interesting contrast to the modern informality of the first class "Monkey Bar" on the present **Oriana**, below, left. At the right, below, is a view of the first officer's stateroom aboard the big P & O cargo liner **Namur** of 1906.

—P & O-ORIENT LINES PHOTO

Above: Deck sports on the motor liner **Dominion Monarch.**

—PHOTO BY ALBERT N. PLUSH

Opposite: S.S. **America** follows Moran tug to her New York pier.

—PHOTO COURTESY OF FRANK O. BRAYNARD

PROW OF S.S. VICTORIA smashing through Bering Sea rollers on her way to Nome.

Opposite Page, above, Alaska Liner **Aleutian** (1), on the Inside Passage.

Opposite Page, below, the great Australian Bight as seen from the **Dominion Monarch.**

Right: S.S. **Stuttgart** passing through the Suez Canal.

VALENCIA embarking passengers before her tragic voyage from San Francisco.

WRECK OF VALENCIA

Shortly after the turn of the century a San Francisco newspaper editorialized bitterly: *"The passenger ships of the Pacific Coast are with few exceptions so rotten that the least accident crushes them like eggshells and sends them to the bottom. The vessels used on this coast are the cast-offs from the East Coast, where they have been practically worn out and are sold for a song to the Pacific shipping companies. There are only six really safe passenger ships on the Pacific, four trans-Pacific liners belonging to the Pacific Mail Steamship Company, the* Minnesota *and the coastwise liner* President. *Most of the passenger ships of this coast are so old that one can throw a rivet hammer through them"*.

There was considerable truth to the complaint, particularly following the flood of superannuated shipping which flocked to the West Coast during the great Alaska gold rush of 1897. One such was the old iron-hulled single-screw liner *Valencia*, which went into Seattle-Alaska service following a tour of duty as a Spanish War transport. In January, 1906, the Pacific Coast Steamship Company diverted her temporarily to the San Francisco-Vancouver, Canada-Puget Sound run. She sailed north from the Golden Gate on the morning of January 11, 1906.

Visibility was poor on her northward voyage. Captain Johnson was forced to rely on dead reackoning. Both the sounding machine and the log were in operation, but both were unreliable; the patent log had been known to "overrun" the ship by as much as six percent. A strong northerly current and south wind were setting the steamer further north than the captain's best calculations indicated.

Already past the broad, safe mouth of the Strait of Juan de Fuca, the old *Valencia* blundered onto the reef-fanged coast of the ship's graveyard of Vancouver Island and was forced broadside against a sheer cliff too high to scale. While would-be rescue craft kept a death-watch off shore, the *Valencia's* people lashed themselves in the rigging as the great North Pacific breakers smashed the old iron hull to fragments. For a while they watched the helpless rescue ships and sang *Nearer My God to Thee;* then they began dying one by one.

A few escaped in lifeboats and rafts to be picked up by the waiting ships, but of the 154 who sailed from San Francisco on the *Valencia,* 117 died in the pounding surf of the Vancouver Island reef where she struck and disintegrated.

Afterward it was difficult to recover the bodies of the victims. Although most wore life-jackets something seemed to weigh them down heavily. Investigation showed the life-jackets were doing it. Filled with tule reeds rather than cork, they soon became saturated and worse than useless. Some of the surviving crew of the *Valencia* testified later that they always carried their own life-jackets, because they knew the ones furnished by the company wouldn't float!

Four years later the Seattle *Times* reported, "*During the past summer persistent reports were brought into Seattle by sailors on vessels frequently in and out of the Cape, of a phantom ship seen off the dangerous coast of Vancouver Island. They said it resembled the ill-fated Valencia, which went down in those waters a few, short years ago with more than 100 souls, and that they could vaguely see human forms clinging to her masts and rigging. On some occasions the spectacle seemed immobile, and again the mystery was accentuated by the fact that the phantom moved steadily with the ship of those who watched, maintaining its relative position perfectly. Again it leaped upon the rocks where the real ship met destruction.*"

The phantom of the *Valencia* has never been fully explained, but surely if ever a ship's company had reason to return as sad wraiths to jog the consciences of those still living the victims of the *Valencia* disaster did.

LIFEBOAT FROM VALENCIA approaching rescue steamer **Queen.**

ACH!

AIR AND SEA RIVALRY of pre-World War I England and Germany was typified by these newspaper cartoons of 1907.

GERMANY--Pretty good, hey?

No Sails Needed . . .

THE CITY OF PARIS

Even if you had known her well in her prime, when she was one of the two most beautiful steamships in the world, you probably wouldn't have recognized the charred, abandoned hulk on the Naples mudflats. Which is just as well, for she was once a lovely ship, a brave, proud ship. That she had come upon evil days was no fault of her own. She lived too long, and shame came upon her in her old age.

* * * * *

A new era began on the North Atlantic when the Clyde-built Inman liner *City of Paris* and her sister ship *City of New York* were launched in 1889 to snatch the Blue Riband from the Cunard racers *Etruria* and *Umbria*. Their beauty could be appreciated even by confirmed wind ship men, for they had the hulls of giant clippers; long and slim and full of grace. Their three slim funnels raked smartly aft, along with their three tall masts, and though they carried no sail, they carried the tapered, questing bowsprits of sailing ships.

They needed no sails, for these were the first successful ocean liners to be driven by twin-screws. If a shaft snapped or a racing propeller dropped off at sea they had power left to bring them into port under steam. Designed to serve as fast auxiliary cruisers in time of war, they had giant triple-expansion engines, which developed 18,500 horsepower and drove them at 20 knots. Even today, more than half a century after they were built, no ship has been designed with a sturdier, safer hull than theirs. Each was equipped with 15 transverse bulkheads which extended right up to the salon deck, 15 feet above the water line. There wasn't an opening in any of the bulkheads. They were solid, waterproof walls of

steel. The builders didn't even take a chance on water-tight doors below the level of the salon deck.

Their slashing passages played havoc with ocean speed records from the start. Early in her career the *City of Paris* made her run in five days, 14 hours, and 24 minutes. Until then it was front page news when a ship made the crossing in less than a full week.

In May of 1890, while knifing eastward toward the Irish coast at full speed, the *City of Paris* broke one of her two propeller shafts. The ship was convulsed from stem to stern with the sudden, unleashed power of the racing engine. Before the steam could be shut off the runaway engine simply whirled itself into sudden ruin. A connecting rod snapped and tore through the engine room like a gigantic projectile, smashing cylinders, wrecking the condenser, and flooding the engine room. Fragments of machinery crashed through the bulkhead between the two engine rooms. Soon the undamaged engine was flooded out too, and the liner lay helpless.

With wireless yet to be invented, there was only one way to bring help to the drifting ship. A lifeboat was lowered and headed toward Ireland. In two days the boat made Queenstown and powerful tugs were soon racing toward the stricken liner. The *City of Paris* was towed into Queenstown just four days late.

Although the Inman Line was owned in the United States, its ships had always flown the British flag. The Congress, in its infinite wisdom, had ruled that only American-built ships could be registered under the American flag. Neither ship owners or citizens were particularly happy about this law, particularly in the case of the beautiful Inman liners. Americans felt they had a right to the full prestige of the great ships which left the best of the European liners wallowing in the wake of their thundering screws. In 1892 a deal was accordingly made which permitted the Inman Line to transfer the two big *City* ships to the American flag, providing two new ships were built in American yards. After that the Inman Line became the American Line, the two racing liners had their names shortened to *New York* and *Paris*.

The *Paris* went to war in 1898 as the auxiliary scouting cruiser *Yale*. She was often under fire, running in close to the Spanish fortifications in Cuba to shell them with her tiny broadside of six-pounders, which were all the Navy could spare her. After the war ended she was returned to her old owners, got her name changed back to *Paris*, and took up her old duties on the Atlantic ferry.

Leaving Southampton in a heavy fog the following year, she suffered a catastrophe that would have finished off a lesser ship. She went hard and fast aground on the Manacles—that treacherous graveyard of hidden rocks off Lands End. Pierced and held fast by the granite fangs of the Manacles, she lay there for almost a month, but she was rescued at last by the salvagers. Towed to port, she was repaired, rebuilt, and renamed *Philadelphia*. Then, in 1900, she went back to work on her old route, holding her own against new luxury liners that were 20 years her junior.

The war of 1917 saw the brave old ship back in navy gray. Renamed the *Harrisburg*, she mounted guns again, and spent the next two years carrying troops to and from France. At the end of her second term of war service she went back to her original owners once more. Her name was changed back to *Philadelphia* and she gamely raced her old course between Southampton and New York.

Her fate was sealed in 1923 when the American Line decided to put her up for sale. She was hopelessly outmoded. She couldn't hope to compete with the *Mauretania* and the *Majestic* and the *Leviathan*. Business is business, and that was that.

And so the grand old *City of Paris* found herself acquired by a fly-by-night "steamship line" of South European ownership; the property of men who had probably changed their names as often as hers had been changed. Old and battered, with rusty paint, and only a hint of her famous beauty left, she tried a cut-rate emigrant service. Her last voyage was a hopeless fiasco. Outbound to Naples the crew mutinied. They hadn't been paid and were fed little enough. With the simple direct action of sailors they tried to take their grudge out on the ship, although she was not to blame for their unhappiness, nor for her own. The crew tried to scuttle the ship; the officers flourished loaded guns. It was in the best tradition of a Hollywood Class-B sea epic, and a sad end for so fine a ship. At Naples the crew set her afire and fled. The charred hulk drifted ashore and lay there a long time, until an Italian junk yard picked her bones.

o   o   o   o

Ships, like men, sometimes live too long. They outlive their usefulness and fall upon evil days. It is kindest to forget the humiliations of their later days and remember them as they were when they made history and their names were legendary. City of Paris was a lovely ship, a brave, proud ship, and she has surely gone wherever it may be that good ships go.

CITY OF PARIS aground off the Manacles, May 20, 1899.
—FRANK O. BRAYNARD PHOTO

THE KAISER'S TREASURE SHIP

Captain Charles Polack, left, who commanded **Kronprinzessin Cecile** on her famous dash to Bar Harbor, was a skilled commander and one of the most popular captains in the history of the trans-Atlantic liners. Among his many medals was one awarded him by the Kaiser for taking the **Kaiser Wilhelm der Grosse** safely through a series of gales, steering her by means of her twin screws after she lost her rudder. He was also decorated by Queen Victoria for saving the crew of a sinking British sailing ship.

The *Doppelschrauben Schnelldampfer*[4] *Kronprinzessin Cecilie* of the Hamburg-American Line's pre-World War I New York express service was a classic example of the ocean greyhound at the turn of the century. She, like the other rakish German four-stackers of that era, was designed on the principal that trans-Atlantic passengers were destined for sea-sickness, but that its ravages should be suffered amid the greatest possible splendor and for the shortest time possible.

[4] Twin-screw Express Steamer.

Schnelldampfer
KRONPRINZESSIN CECILIE

Long, slim and over-powered with their great reciprocating engines, they rolled and pitched drunkenly at the very hint of a sea, vibrating alarmingly as they slashed their way across the North Atlantic at 23 knots and better.

Despite these minor discomforts, *Kronprinzessin Cecilie* was always well patronized by the cream of the trans-Atlantic traveling set in those pre-jet days. The crack Hamburg-American liners were much favored by celebrities, dignitaries and Social Register-ites of the Newport and Bar Harbor set. Ordinary

millionaires, whose wives hoped some day to fight their way into the Social Register followed in the wake of the Great.

The *Kronprinzessin's* master, Captain Polack, helped to make his ship a favorite. He looked the way an ocean liner captain *should* look; tall, broad-shouldered, magnificently mustached and impeccable in his handsome brass-bound uniform. He went well with the rakish four-stacker's "Late North German Lloyd" decor, which Ralph E. Whitney describes in his *Sea Queens in Exile* as "two of everything but the kitchen range and then gilded".

The select clientel of the *Kronprinzessin's* first-class accommodations thought they were setting out on a routine summer crossing in late July of 1914, but it turned out to be anything but that. It developed into a celebrated drama of the sea, replete with famous personalities, a war, a mad dash through darkened seas, the traditional bumbling British Colonel for comic relief . . . and something like twelve million dollars in gold and silver bullion in the ship's strong-room for overseas delivery.

On the fourth night at sea the passengers had departed from the rococo grand dining salon, where they had partaken of delicacies from the ship's tremendous menu beneath the three-decks-high glass dome; or from the ultra plush Vienna Cafes, where one could dine *a la carte*, a really elaborate meal costing about the price of a one-way ticket in the steerage. Some had strayed to the all-male refuge of the *Rauchzimmer* (ladies stayed out of smoking rooms in those innocent days), or to the boat deck to sniff the salty air and the occasional whiffs of coal-smoke from the four towering funnels. Most of them were at the after-dinner dance in the grand salon, but dancing became difficult as the pulse of the great engines seemed to race at a new and disturbing beat. The *Kranprinzessin's* normal jumpiness had become a racking vibration. Then somebody noticed that the moon was on the wrong side of the ship. The speeding liner had reversed her course!

Captain Polack descended majestically from the bridge to announce that war was about to be declared between the Central and Allied Powers; that *Kronprinzessin Cecilie* was headed, with her multi-million-dollar treasure, back for the neutral safety of the United States. All electric lights were to be extinguished. No wireless messages were to be sent.

Some of the first-class passengers were delighted. Here was sea adventure worthy of the rakish, hell-for-leather express liner. Others, to whom time was money, were deeply annoyed. A group of American business tycoons pooled their ready cash and made an offer to Captain Polack to buy the *Kronprinzessin Cecilie*, hoist the United States colors and *dare* the

British Navy to open fire. Captain Polack refused the offer politely. The British Colonel engaged in a long altercation with the other passengers most of whom were, at that time, highly pro-German. When the lights went out a woman in the steerage tried to jump overboard.

Next day a paint crew was ordered out by Captain Polack to paint black bands at the top of the four yellow funnels, the idea being to disguise the *Kronprinzessin* as the British four-funneled *Olympic*. The painters suffered great discomfort as they worked on the hot funnels amid clouds of acrid coal-smoke on what was, at best, a feeble *ruse de guerre*. It would have been a naive British naval officer indeed who could not tell the slim German liner with her distinctively paired funnels from the beamy bulk of the *Olympic*.

The liner raced on to her mysterious destination, thereafter through heavy fog, but with lights still extinguished and foghorn silent. Passengers stayed awake, dressed and wearing life preservers. More and more of them were agreeing with the critical opinions of the British Colonel. Delegations approached Captain Polack requesting that he get things back to normal. The urbane commander, who had been in the wireless room listening to the air crackling with hostile inquiries as to his ship's whereabouts, remained polite but firm.

On the morning of August 4, 1914, the residents of the posh resort town of Bar Harbor awoke wonderingly to see a huge ocean liner towering above their yachts and sailboats in the harbor. The counterfeit White Star funnel markings fooled *them*, and word spread that *Olympic*, sister-ship to the late *Titanic*, was anchored at Bar Harbor. Soon the error was corrected, and when the evening editions of the New York papers came aboard, the passengers of the *Kronprinzessin Cecilie* found that they were all celebrities now. The whole world had been wondering what had happened to the "German Gold Ship".

They stopped preparing letters of censure about Captain Polack and presented him instead with a resolution praising his skill and courage.

Kronprinzessin Cecilie stayed at Bar Harbor for the season, as did the dashing Captain Polack, without whose presence no really correct function was complete. In the winter the big liner was towed to Boston, staying carefully inside the three-mile limit, to the frustration of the British cruisers which patrolled offshore.

Her glory days were ended. When America entered the war the old *schnelldampfer* became the U. S. transport *Mt. Vernon* and, as such, she lost all her admirers. The American soldiers who crossed on her referred to her as *Vermin,* while the Kaiser's govern-

HOT WORK for crew was repainting of four funnels in effort to camouflage **Cecilie.**

ment put a price on her head with a standing offer of an Iron Cross to the U-boat commander who should sink her. None of them did.

After the war she lay for years in shabby lay-up on the Patuxent River in company with her old fleet-mate *Kaiser Wilhelm II* and the stodgier ex-Hamburg-American liners *America* (ex-*Amerika*) and *George Washington*. From there the venerable ocean greyhound went to the scrapping yards just before America's entry into the second World War.

Had she been reprieved a bit longer the *Kronprinzessin Cecilie* might have written a new chapter of sea melodrama in a new war.

GLIDING THROUGH the tranquil waters of Norway's Geirander Fjord, the Swedish-American cruise liner **Gripsholm,** opposite page, proves that she is indeed one of the world's most beautiful ships. More important from an economic standpoint, she's also one of the most popular among discriminating voyagers.

—SWEDISH-AMERICAN LINE PHOTO

COLLISION
AT SEA

Among the many hazards of the sea which are always present to bring disaster down upon the head of the unwary or unskilled navigator, the risk of collision with another ship, or with inanimate floating objects such as derelicts or icebergs, is always present. Wartime, with its crowded harbors and vast convoys, multiplies this danger many times. One of the most spectacular and tragic collisions of World War II was the ramming of the British cruiser *Curacoa* by the gigantic Cunard flagship *Queen Mary*.

This long-suppressed sea tragedy took place in October of 1942, witnessed by thousands of British and American Army and Navy personnel, but it remained a closely guarded secret for the next five years.

On that autumn morning the mighty *Queen* came sweeping in from the Atlantic toward the Irish coast, her cabins, holds and decks jammed with 15,000 American troops bound for the North African invasion. As always, she had crossed the Atlantic alone, relying on her speed to escape submarines and surface raiders.

As she neared the Bloody Foreland, Captain Illingworth kept anxious watch from her towering bridge. The German bombers specialized in pouncing on ships emerging from the trackless ocean to become easy pickings in restricted coastal waters; the killing of the *Queen Mary* would make a national hero of the U-boat skipper or bomber pilot who did the job.

Off the Foreland *Queen Mary* was joined by the light antiaircraft cruiser *Curacoa*, which came rolling and pitching out to meet her through moderately heavy seas which had little effect on the great *Queen*. Ahead, over the horizon, a half dozen swift destroyers coursed like hounds to pick up any scent of lurking U-boats. The *Queen Mary* was among friends again.

The *Queen Mary* retained her normal wartime cruising speed of 28 knots and continued on her zig-zag course down the Irish coast toward the Clyde estuary. *Curacoa* had frequently convoyed the *Queen* on this last leg of her voyages and her cammander, Captain John Boutwood, knew the routine. Captain Boutwood's orders were succinct; *"Protect Queen Mary at all costs"*.

The *Curacoa* was an old light cruiser of World

War 1 vintage converted in 1939 to a fast-moving platform for antaircraft guns, with which she fairly bristled. Her 40,000-horsepower geared turbines and twin-screws were designed to give her a top speed of 29 knots, but with more than twenty years of hard service behind her, and in the steep, choppy seas, she was hard-pressed to maintain station close alongside the *Queen*. The little cruiser of only 4,200 tons displacement pitched and rolled and panted oil smoke from her twin funnels. The *Queen Mary* strode through the sea with all the majestic power of her more than eighty-thousand tons.

By noon the cruiser was laboring hard and Captain Boutwood decided to maintain a straight-line course, steering close astern of the *Queen* as she maintained her zig-zag pattern. At two o'clock, with the new procedure apparently working well, the *Queen's* captain felt safe in leaving the bridge long enough for a delayed lunch. He turned the bridge over temporarily to Junior First Officer Wright, who in turn was relieved in a few minutes by Chief Officer Robinson. Their orders were clear; maintain course and speed. It was up to the experienced naval crew of the *Curacoa* to keep out of the sea giant's way.

As Chief Officer Robinson took over on the bridge, *Queen Mary* was heeling almost imperceptably to begin a starboard turn. *Curacoa* was about two cable-lengths ahead, just off the liner's bow. The distance, a little over twice the *Queen Mary's* length seemed adequate. *Curacoa* had been shaving it much closer than that.

Then, suddenly, there was no sea-room at all. The cruiser appeared to swing broadside right under the *Queen's* onrushing prow. On the cruiser's bridge Captain Boutwood and the officers and ratings on watch had a brief, nightmare glimpse of the liner's bows towering above them like a moving mountain. Then H. M. S. *Curacoa's* death-scream sounded . . . the scream of tortured steel and bursting seams. The great prow of the *Queen Mary* cut through the cruiser's hull of three-inch armored steel and swept on at undiminished speed. The broken halves of the cruiser bobbed like driftwood in the whirlpool of the giant's passing. In minutes the severed remains sank, leaving only a cloud of drifting steam from the smashed boilers and a few human dots rising and falling with the sea.

The officers on the liner's bridge stared in horror at the destruction their ship had left. The horror seemed greater because the *Queen* had not faltered or trembled at the impact. The troops below, enjoying a farewell steak dinner, weren't even aware that anything had happened. There was an air of unreality about this most shocking sea tragedy of the war.

Captain Illingworth kept his ship on her ordained course at undiminished speed. The code of war superceded the ancient code of the sea. The irreplaceable Queen, her 15,000 fighting men and the thousand skilled merchant seamen of her crew must be delivered safe on the Clyde. No other consideration was possible. Wireless messages brought destroyers slashing out to search for survivors, but of the *Curacoa's* crew of nearly 450 men, only 101 naval ratings and one officer were saved. The only officer to survive the nightmare destruction of the cruiser was her commander, Captain Boutwood.

Inspection showed that the *Queen Mary's* only damage was a slight break in her stem and the loss of a bit of paint. It was awesome proof of the unbelievable power and strength of a great ocean liner moving at high speed.

Fortunately not many of the wartime collisions approached the *Curacoa* disaster in loss of life; some of them even had their overtones of comedy. The 20,000-ton Cunard intermediate liner *Samaria* of 1921 vintage found herself, in the course of her World War II trooping duties, sandwiched between the huge Cunard four-stacker *Aquitania* and the British aircraft carrier

Furious while at anchor off Halifax, Nova Scotia. The roadstead was jammed with ships preparing to form a convoy, among them *Empress of Britain* and *Empress of Australia,* all with American troops aboard.

Those on the bridge of the 600-foot *Samaria* were horrified to suddenly discern the 900-foot bulk of *Aquitania* under way and looming high above their starboard side. The bridge watch barely had time to flee to the doubtful shelter of the chart-room when the pondeously moving bulk of the *Acquitania* swept along *Samaria's* starboard side. The bridge wing was crumpled up like cardboard, half the *Samaria's* outswung lifeboats were swept away in kindling and a heavy antiaircraft gun turret was knocked from the top of the bridge and lodged against the upper deckhouse. The *Samaria's* captain, horrified at the sounds of destruction, found the door from his quarters jammed shut by the toppled gun turret. Unable to get out and see what was going on, he suspected the worst.

Seconds later another huge shape loomed high above the poor *Samaria's* port side. H. M. S. *Furious* was also under way and she proceeded to do to *Samaria's* port side exactly what the *Aquitania* had done to the starboard!

When a rescue party reached the *Samaria's* master his orders were brief and to the point. "Let's get the bloody hell out of here".

Which is exactly what the *Samaria* did.

Then there is the classic case of the Canadian Pacific three-stacker *Empress of Australia,* benighted in the midst of a heavy Atlantic fog and strayed from the rest of her convoy, of which the *Aquitania* was serving as flagship. When the convoy arrived at its rendezvous point there was much concern over the fate of the missing *Empress,* but as the fog lifted she was seen standing in toward the rest of the fleet.

As she approached, a signal-hoist climbed to the yard-arm of the escorting British cruiser. Those on the bridge of the *Aquitania* tried to read it, but it just didn't seem to make sense. Suddenly Captain Gibbons shouted for a copy of the Bible to be brought to the bridge. The signal seemed to consist only of book, chapter and verse.

It took some time to locate a copy of the Good Book, during which interval the *Aquitania's* flag remained at a prolonged half-dip, indicating that the cruiser's signal was "not understood".

Finally a Bible was located and rushed to the bridge. Captain Gibbons shuffled quickly through the pages to the indicated lines and the cruiser's message referring to the *Empress of Australia* became clear:

"And lo—the lost lamb is found."

Death of Andrea Doria

On the night of July 25, 1956, the Italian Line's newest luxury liner, the 697- foot *Andrea Doria* was approaching Nantucket Lightship at the close of her 4,000-mile westward crossing from Genoa for New York. Also approaching the lightship, but outward-bound from New York were the French Line's big *Isle de France* and the Swedish-American Line's *Stockholm*, 525-foot motorship placed in service in 1948 as the first new liner to cross the Atlantic after World War II. The two latter ships had left port at about the same time, but *Isle de France,* working up to her 24-knot speed, was fast pulling away from the 17-knot *Stockholm.*

At about 9:30 p.m., having passed Nantucket light-ship and set course for Ambrose lightship, the watch officer at the *Andrea Doria's* radar picked up the image of another ship moving toward them at a distance of seventeen miles. The *Stockholm's* radar picked up the "pip" of the *Andrea Doria* when the two ships were still twelve miles apart. They main-tained radar contact continuously thereafter, until visual contact was made at a distance of about two

miles. It appeared to the officers on the *Andrea Doria's* bridge that the two ships would pass safely, starboard to starboard.

But suddenly the illusion of distance was shattered. Captain Calamai on the *Andrea Doria's* bridge real-ized too late that his ship was on collision course and that she was closing with the oncoming stranger at a combined speed of nearly forty miles an hour. The Italian liner's wheel was spun to port, but too late. A 30,000-ton ship does not skid into a turn like a racing car. The two liners came together, both with engineroom telegraphs set at "Full Ahead".

The smaller *Stockholm* was equipped with a heavily reinforced ice-breaker bow for Arctic navigation. Combining the attributes of both a battering ram and a butcher's cleaver on a huge scale, the raking white prow smashed deep into the *Andrea Doria's* starboard side. As the graceful Italian liner heeled drunkenly under the impact, the white shape of the *Stockholm* drifted off into the night, her slim bows crushed into a blunt tangle of wreckage.

Although only one compartment of the *Andrea Doria's hull* was open to the sea, the beautiful sea queen lay over on her right side like a dying thing. The stability was gone from her eleven-story high fabric and the list grew progressively worse until the sea rushed into her and claimed her.

The *Isle de France* came looming grandly out of the night in answer to the distress calls, her name emblazoned above the sea in giant electric lights after the manner of ships of the French Line. Her boats and those of the *Stockholm* saved all but 43 of the 1,706 souls aboard the *Andrea Doria*, for that lovely ship was a long time dying.

In number of lives lost the *Andrea Doria-Stockholm* collision was not a major sea disaster but it was a spectacular one, and certainly the most puzzling and controversial one in maritime history.

Exactly why it happened is almost as much a mystery today as on the clear, or hazy or foggy night the *Stockholm* and the *Andrea Doria* tried to pass starboard to starboard (or was it port to port?) and met, instead, in collision at sea.

NEXT PAGE: AWESOME BOW of the mighty **Queen Mary,** shown here in drydock, sliced through the British cruiser **Curacoa** like a knife through butter.

—CUNARD LINE PHOTOS

Proud Queen Of The Seas In Her Death Struggle

LUXURY LINER ANDREA DORIA KEELS FAR OVER AS SHE BEGINS FINAL PLUNGE TO SEA'S FLOOR. ARROW SHOWS WHERE BOW OF STOCKHOLM CUT INTO HER.
—(Copyright by Boston Traveler, 1956, via Associated Press Wirephoto.)

THE STRICKEN LINER QUIETLY ROLLS ON ITS SIDE
The Unused Lifeboats On Their Davits Break Off

SLOWLY, THE HUGE LINER GOES DOWN BY THE BOW.

Headed Back To New York

HELICOPTER HOVERS over the stern of the Swedish liner Stockholm to take off injured as the liner slowly limps back to New York after the collision in a thick fog with the Italian liner Andrea Doria 45 miles south of Nantucket Island. The Stockholm with its crushed bow is carrying 425 survivors of the tragedy, plus 750 passengers of its own.
—(Associated Press Wirephoto.)

Andrea Doria's Final Moments

THIS DRAMATIC series of pictures shows the last moments of the sinking Italian liner Andrea Doria as she went down off Nantucket Island Thursday after the collision with the Swedish liner Stockholm. The unused lifeboats break away (upper left) as the ship rolls over on her side. Water boils about the stern, the propeller shows and debris strews the water as the liner goes under. And nothing is left but bubbling water, oil and litter on the face of the sea as the Andrea Doria sinks to her grave. These photos are copyrighted by Boston Traveler.
—(Associated Press Wirephoto.)

MOTOR LINER STOCKHOLM

ANDREA DORIA'S starboard list gradually increased until she rolled over on her side and sank.

—U. S. COAST GUARD PHOTO

TWIN SUPER LINERS **Michelangelo** and **Raffaello,** scheduled to enter trans-Atlantic service in 1964, demonstrate Italian Line's flair for pleasingly advanced ship design without the freakish appearance that has caused some of the "new look" liners to be criticized as looking "like a block of flats." Although streamlined and functional, these all-white beauties are unmistakably ships.
—ITALIAN LINE DRAWING

NOTEWORTHY ADDITION to faltering U.S. Merchant Marine of the 1890's were the twin American Line steamers **St. Louis** and **St. Paul,** above. Built in 1895 in the American yard of Cramp & Sons at Philadelphia, their construction being a stipulation by Congress upon granting U.S. registry to **City of New York** (New York) and **City of Paris** (Philadelphia). The 11,629-ton, 535-foot liners served as transports in World War I. **St. Louis** as the **Louisville,** and **St. Paul** as the **Knoxville. St. Louis** was scrapped in Italy in 1925. **St. Paul** preceding her by two years to the yards of German shipbreakers.

—FRANK O. BRAYNARD PHOTO

EMPRESSES, OLD AND NEW

THE 5,905-TON EMPRESS OF CHINA, above, was one of the original fleet of three "White Empresses" which inaugurated trans-Pacific service by Canadian Pacific-owned vessels. The first large twin-screw vessels on the Pacific, they maintained their fame and popularity well into the 20th century.

SPLENDID NEW FLAGSHIP of the Canadian Pacific fleet is the twin-screw turbine liner **Empress of Canada,** below, pictured in the harbor of Montreal, from which she sails in Atlantic service with her twin sisters **Empress of England** and **Empress of Britain.** The **Empress of Canada,** a 650-foot ship of 27,300 gross tons, was launched from the Walker on Tyne yard of Vickers Armstrongs (Shipbuilders) Ltd. Her maiden voyage from Liverpool to Quebec and Montreal via Greenock was made in April, 1961.
—CANADIAN PACIFIC PHOTOS

STRANGEST SEA STORY EVER TOLD

Morgan Robertson was a merchant seaman in the turn-of-the-century days of comfortless, crowded foc'sles, scant and grudging food and even scantier pay, but Robertson was different in at least one respect from his hard-bitten comrades. Instead of the traditional amusements of the deep-sea sailor, Morgan Robertson spent his spare time writing.

Over the years he accumulated a trunkfull of manuscripts, stories of the sea mostly, and a fine collection of rejection slips from editors all over the world. Morgan Robertson lived and died a poor seafaring man and that most frustrated of all striving humanity . . . an unpublished author.

After his death, his widow came across the trunk in the attic stuffed full of Robertson's unpublished manuscripts. She began reading them, thought them good, and took up her husband's quest for a publisher. She was more successful than her husband and the sea tales of Morgan Robertson filled a whole set of books.

One of the stories published after his death may well be the strangest sea story ever told.

It is the story of a great, four-funnel ocean liner built in England as the world's largest ship, the ultimate in sea-going luxury. This great ship set out from Southampton on her maiden voyage carrying the elite of two continents. The world marveled at her vast size . . . over 800 feet in length and of more than 45,000 tons.

On her westward voyage across the Atlantic her captain was harried by company officials anxious for a fast passage to bring her further fame. Off the Newfoundland Banks the speeding liner crashed into a huge ice berg. As the water rushed into her slashed hull it was realized too late that there were not enough lifeboats to carry her passengers and crew. Most of the ship's company died in the icy waters of the North Atlantic.

The name of the great ocean liner which collided with an ice berg on her maiden voyage from Southampton to New York and sank with such terrible loss of life was, in Robertson's story, R.M.S. *Titan*.

So what's strange about this tale of the sea? you ask. Obviously he simply took the tragic drama of R.M.S. *Titanic* ,dropped a couple of letters from her name and then reproduced the story of her building, her specifications, her sailing and her grim fate . . .exactly as they happened. Scores of writers since 1912 have based plays and stories on the *Titanic*.

True, Morgan Robertson simply wrote about the *Titanic*, accurately in almost every detail, except for the omission of those last two letters in her name.

The strange thing is that he told the story of the *Titanic* disaster, exactly as it happened . . . *ten years before the* Titanic *was launched*.

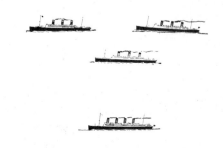

PROTOTYPE OF THE Orient Line's post-World War I class of 20,000-ton turbine liners, the **Ormonde,** pictured above in full dress as flagship of the 1931 Anniversary Regatta at Sydney, was laid down at John Brown and Company's Clydebank yard in 1913, but her building was delayed by the first World War and she was not completed until 1917. When she was designed she was the largest ship planned with geared turbines, and the more conservative company officials favored the triple-screw combination of reciprocating and turbine engines of her predecessor, **Orama** of 1911. Her compound turbines of 15,000 shaft horsepower proved efficient, however, giving her a service speed of 18 knots on the Australian run. In 1932 she was altered to carry 770 passengers in all tourist-class accomodations, and in 1947 she was converted to an austerity emigrant carrier, carrying more than 18,000 new settlers from Great Britain to Australia during the next five years, 1,052 to a voyage. Late in 1952 she completed her 75th and last round voyage to Australia. She was a popular ship with passengers and crews alike, and when she departed Tilbury for the last time, every ship in Gravesend Reach saluted her with the traditional three farewell whistle-blasts. —P & O-ORIENT LINES PHOTO

JAUNTY CRUISE LINER Brittany, lower r i g h t, presented a pretty picture as she steamed from New York for seven-d a y cruises to Bermuda a n d N a s s a u, but her glory days have ended. In e a r l y A p r i l, 1963 she caught fire while undergoing repairs at a Pireaus shipyard, is reported a total loss. She was flagship of Caribbean Cruise Lines with headquarters at Washington, D. C. She had been replaced f o r the 1963-1964 season by the French liner **Provence.**

Farcial Finish of a
FAMOUS SHIP

There has never been a sea disaster like the one that ended the career of the French Line's great flagship Isle de France off Osaka, Japan in 1959. In the course of the fine old ship's humiliation a beautiful blonde named Dorothy Malone struggled with her water-logged false eyelashes while her husband, Robert Stack, struggled to remove her from under a mass of wreckage which pinned her knee-deep in her flooded stateroom. The French Liner's Japanese captain was knocked down by a fire hose, stewards stood about sullenly muttering "Damn Yankee" while, below decks, bulkheads gave way and tons of water surged through the engine room, and passengers diving overboard screamed horribly as they were stung by jellyfish, while a noted American film producer capered happily about the liner's huge forward stack, which had fallen down and smashed the captain's quarters.

Isle de France had entered the Atlantic luxury trade in 1927 as the French Line's pride; for more than twenty years her name was synonymous with beauty, luxury and glamor. When she was sold, in 1959, to an Osaka scrapyard, she was given a sentimental *adieu* from La Havre by hundreds of misty-eyed admirers and a band playing the *Marseillaise*. Only after she left the harbor was the tricolor replaced by the Japanese ensign and her new name, *Furanzu* (France) *Maru*, unveiled.

France and the French Line were horrified when it was discovered that the Japanese Junkies had turned over the lovely *Isle* to a Hollywood producer for $4,000.00 a day as a floating prop for the film "Last Voyage." There were screams of outrage and threats of law suits from many quarters, but all the awful things described above happened to the poor old *Isle de France*, and more. Finally this sad victim of movie realism, her forward funnel gone and her interior a shambles, was turned over to the scrapyard for merciful oblivion.

All of which may help to explain why, in 1962, Shaw-Savill refused to allow *its* retiring flagship *Dominion Monarch* to be used by American film-makers at any price.

NORMANDIE'S
EXTRA WHISTLE

SKILLED SKIPPERS of these veteran Moran docking tugs wondered if **Normandie's** pilot had gone whistle-happy.
—MORAN TOWING & TRANSPORTATION CO. PHOTO

In the depths of the great depression of the 1930's the **French Line** had invested more than eighty million dollars in 83,423 tons of beauty, speed and luxury named *Normandie*. Product of the Penhoet yards at St. Nazaire, this tremendous ship was the first in the world to exceed a thousand feet in length. On her maiden voyage, in June of 1935, her 160,000-horsepower turbines sent her knifing across the Atlantic at almost thirty knots to take the legendary Blue Riband.

New York waited to welcome her on the perfect summer day of June 2. At noon, as the great ship steamed majestically up the bay,[1] bedlam broke loose. Ticker-tape showered down from the skyscrapers inland, whistles blasted their welcome to the new queen of the seas. Planes and blimps droned overhead and dipped to drop flowers on the liner's deck. A flotilla of smaller craft escorted *Normandie* past spouting fireboats. Close alongside puffed twelve Moran harbor tugs assigned to dock her. On her bridge the docking pilot, Captain Anton Huseby, stood with the harbor pilot and the liner's master, Captain Rene Pugnet. It would be Huseby's delicate task to guide the vast bulk of the *Normandie* into her slip.

The pilot and the tugs faced a monumental task. The minimum depth of the Hudson River below her berth was 40 feet; *Normandie* was drawing over 38 feet. The tugs had, at times, to literally push the great keel through the mud and silt of the river bottom.

The great ship slipped past the rusting and deserted *Leviathan* and angled toward her 48th Street pier. Twelve straining tugs beat the water to a froth as their masters responded to the shrill blasts of pilot Huseby's police whistle. Then *Normandie's* sheer bulk took over, drifting momentarily out of control toward the pier. Quickly Huseby ordered her backed out, the bow line was made fast to a winch on the pier and she was warped in a foot at a time.

What had caused the momentary confusion of the veteran skippers? Captain Huseby had wondered about that, too. The mystery was solved by one of the *Normandie's* petty officers.

While the prestige of the world's greatest ocean liner hung in the balance, he found a small boy on the boat deck happily blowing a toy whistle in imitation of the docking pilot on the bridge!

[1]There was nothing "mythical" about *Normandie's* Blue Riband. She made her entrance flying from her masthead an azure pennant a yard long for each knot she had cut from the trans-Atlantic record.

The Liners at War . . .

RAWALPINDI and JERVIS BAY

The merchant ship has traditionally gone to war to fight its country's battles, adding countless chapters to the brave annals of the sea from the days of the Spanish Armada to World War II and the dawn of the nuclear age. It is impossible to list even the names of the liners which distinguished themselves on both sides in two world wars, let alone recount their exploits in detail, but this is the story of two brave ships whose names will not soon be forgotten.

Rawalpindi was summoned to war with the receipt by P & O officials of the brusquely worded Admiralty telegram, "Your vessel *Rawalpindi* is hereby requisitioned for Government service." The telegram was received on August 24, 1939. By November 23 the 16,600-ton P & O Liner was in sea-stained fighting gray, manned by Royal Navy and Naval Reserve men, fitted out with eight old six-inch guns, and on watch for German surface shipping as a unit of the Northern Patrol which guarded the approaches to the North Sea.

The short November day on the North Atlantic was ending in mist and shadow when *Rawalpindi* sighted a big ship looming in the distant haze. Captain E. C. Kennedy reported her by wireless at 3:51 p.m. as an "enemy battle cruiser"; later he decided it was the German battleship *Deutschland*.

Actually it was the mighty *Scharnhorst,* 26,000-ton battle cruiser capable of 30 knots speed and armed with nine 11-inch and twelve 5.9-inch high velocity naval guns. Only three of the British Navy's greatest fighting ships were conceded an even match against the *Scharnhorst* and the little *Rawalpindi* wasn't one of them. Built in 1925, unarmored, with a top speed of 17 knots and armed with her ancient and unreliable guns, a fight between the armored giant and this light merchant cruiser was as hopeless a one as can be conceived of.

Then a British lookout sighted another great shape looming in the fog. It was *Gneisenau,* sister-ship to *Scharnhorst* and equally powerful. As the odds were reported doubled, Captain Kennedy issued his orders . . . *"We'll fight them both."*

Almost immediately one of *Rawalpindi's* ancient guns scored a direct hit amidships on the towering *Gneisenau.* Then the murky air was filled with the scream of the German 11-inch shells. *Rawalpindi* was literally blown to pieces. Fire control communications

P & O LINER RAWALPINDI stood up to 26,000-ton German battle cruisers **Scharnhorst** and **Gneisenau.**

went out as the bridge was shattered and direct hits stopped the main dynamos in the engine room. The remaining British guns fired independently from the inferno of the burning liner until, at 4:15, with her captain dead and the last gun blasted out of action, the gallant *Rawalpindi* was silent and sinking.

For fourteen minutes she had stood up against the two most powerful battle cruisers in the world. In those few minutes the little old *Rawalpindi* earned immortality for herself and her brave crew.[5]

It was almost a year later, on October 28, 1940, that the armed merchant cruiser *Jervis Bay,* late of the Shaw-Savill owned Aberdeen & Commonwealth Line fleet, sailed from Halifax as sole escort of a 38-ship convoy which included the New Zealand Shipping Company's 17,000-ton liner *Rangitiki* and ten loaded tankers. Like the *Rawalpindi, Jervis Bay* had become a warship by the mounting on her of eight discarded Navy six-inch guns.

On the evening of November 5 the convoy was steaming in nine columns abreast, *Jervis Bay* in the center. At four o'clock, smoke was made out on the darkening horizon. Then the German battleship *Admiral Scheer* came charging in like a wolf attacking a flock of sheep. At ten miles distance the orange

[5]Six months after *Rawalpindi* died in the North Atlantic her motorboats, stowed at Tilbury Docks at the time of her conversion, were put in service ferrying British troops back from the bloody beaches of Dunkirk. With the gallant name of *Rawalpindi* at their bows they helped to write another chapter in the history of the war.

flames blossomed at the muzzles of her 11-inch rifles. Two salvoes threw up deadly fountains in the center of the convoy. Signals from *Jervis Bay* ordered the unarmed ships to scatter as she turned and steamed out to meet the *Admiral Scheer.*

The unique German "pocket battleship", of 12,000 tons displacement, was powered by eight M.A.N. diesels of 6,750-horsepower each, was protected by four inches of armor and was rated, with her batteries of 11 and 5.9-inch guns as equal in strength of the battle cruisers which had shattered *Rawalpindi.*

Jervis Bay was smaller and older than *Rawalpindi,* a 14,000-ton steamer built in 1922, but she and her crew were made of the same stuff. Steaming straight for the blasting guns of the battleship, she diverted the full might of the *Admiral Scheer* against herself. Captain Fegan fell mortally wounded on the bridge as *Jervis Bay,* like *Rawalpindi* lay down to die with her last gun silenced, ablaze in twenty places.

Jervis Bay was dead but the ships of her convoy were scattered; no longer sitting ducks for the German raider. Tough Captain Sven Olander turned his Swedish freighter *Stureholm* and picked up the remnants of the gallant crew of *Jervis Bay.*

Only five of the 36 ships were sunk by the *Admiral Scheer* after she had finished with *Jervis Bay.* The rest had been given the precious time they needed to make good their escape.

LIBERTE AT LE HAVRE undergoing conversion after World War II.

S.S. Liberte

FINEST FOOD AFLOAT

As when all great ocean liners retire from their glamorous life to oblivion in the scrapyard, there was sadness when the grand old *Liberte,* once the Blue Riband-winning North German Lloyd *Europa,* retired from French Line service in 1962.

Shipping men and ship enthusiasts recalled her as a giant step forward in the design of fast, luxurious ocean steamships. They admired her long career under two flags throughout a generation of service, always a top contender among the elite of the North Atlantic.

But in the case of the *Liberte* most people who knew her seemed more concerned with the dissolution of her legendary eating facilities than with that of the ship herself. It's difficult to think about the *Liberte* without thinking of your stomach.

More than one hundred and fifty lesser chefs and assistants staffed the great galleys of the *Liberte* under that culinary artist Andre Papion. First-class passengers were known to gain an average of a pound a day in working through the twenty or thirty mouth-watering items on the daily menu. Seasoned *Liberte* voyagers tended to concentrate on such exquisite specialties of the ship as *Filet de Sole Liberte* served in a tantalizing mousee of champagne, *Cotes de Veau Dauphinoise,* and that magical mixture of seafoods in wine sauce called *Gourmandise de Homard Bonne Bouche.*

Roger Angell, writing in *Holiday* magazine, observed that "Gourmets aboard the French liner *Liberte* often conclude that the ship is merely a seagoing enclosure for one of the world's greatest restaurants." Joseph Wechsberg, describing the superb culinary accomplishments of *Liberte* in *Esquire,* was in full agreement. "One of the world's greatest restaurants moves across the Atlantic at an average speed of twenty-four knots", he wrote.

Joe David Brown, a man obviously on the side of the angels (he insists that passenger ships represent the last truly civilized method of travel), was moved to write *Love Song to the Liberte* for *Sports Illustrated* after making a farewell voyage aboard her just before the end. "On no ship was good cooking such a tradition", he wrote, "Was the ordering and preparation of meals such a ritual, and the art of gastronomy such a topic of conversation as it was on the *Liberte.*"

THIS VIEW OF LIBERTE in drydock displays bulbous bow which was one of the innovations given her by her German builders to increase her speed and insure capture of the Atlantic Blue Riband from **Mauretania.**

THIS VIEW OF LIBERTE'S engine room shows part of the vast array of oil-fired boilers which fed steam to her mighty turbines.

On the *Liberte* everyone was willing to take time for a discussion of good eating . . . and drinking; not just the dedicated artists of the steward's department, some of whom had served on the old four-stackers *France* and *Paris,* but *everyone,* from Captain Ferrenbach and Chief Purser Robert Bellet on down. The French were horrified, upon taking over the *Europa* for conversion to *Liberte,* to find that she had no wine cellar. That was immediately rectified, for what is fine food without wine? *Liberte* had one of the finest floating wine cellars in the world.

Ocean liner critics were not agreed that the rococo splendor of *Liberte's* ornate interior typified the best in ship decor, there being those who prefer the wood paneled, polished brass elegance of the British liners, or the chaste simplicity of the modern American and Italian ships. But on one point almost everyone was in agreement.

The food on *Liberte* was just simply wonderful.

LIBERTE'S MAIN DINING SALON, above, was one of the most elegant afloat. Following pages: First Class Menu from **Liberte** was a gourmet's delight.

—FRENCH LINE PHOTO

BELOW, Captain Charles Ferrenbach, last commander of the **Liberte.**

—FRENCH LINE PHOTO

Dîner

HORS-D'ŒUVRE

Beurre de la Manche
Olives Vertes - Olives Noires - Céleri en Branche
Caviar Givré de Russie
Huîtres Fines de Marennes - Salade Caprice
Terrine de Pigeonneau Truffée
Poire d'Avocat à la Cubaine

POTAGES

Velouté de Petits Pois aux Croûtons
Consommé Royale
Potage Garbure à l'Oignon Gratiné au Gruyère

ŒUFS

Œufs Pochés Héloïse
Œufs Plat à la Turque

POISSONS

Turbot de Dieppe Poché Sauce Mousseline
Bar du Golfe de Gascogne Froid Génoise

ENTRÉE

Côte de Charolais Maraîchère

LEGUMES

Artichaut Violet Tiède à l'Huile Douce
Epinards Frais aux Fleurons
Cœur de Céleri Braisé Demi-Glace
Risotto à l'Espagnole
Pommes Idaho au Four - Pommes Vapeur
Pommes Gaufrettes - Pommes Copeaux

PATES

Nouillettes Sicilienne

ROTI

Dindonneau du Languedoc aux Marrons de Naples

GRILLADE
(10 Minutes)

Selle d'Agneau de Béhague Grillée à la Braise

BUFFET FROID

Jambon d'York - Jambon de Virginie Clouté aux Girofles
Jambon de Westphalie - Jambon de Parme
Longe de Veau Mayonnaise - Langue Fumée de Cambrai
Gigot d'Agneau Sauce Menthe
Carré de Porc au Raifort
Poulet de Grain à la Gelée
Terrine de Foie Gras Truffé du Quercy

SALADES

Salade de Chicorée au Roquefort
Cœur de Salade Romaine Louisette
Salade Marie-Stuart

FROMAGES

Tête de Maure - Demi-Sel - Roquefort
Selles-sur-Cher

ENTREMETS

La Coupe Glacée Monte-Cristo
Glace Café
Crème Régence au Chocolat
Bavaroise au Nougat
Cornet Crème au Kirsch
Friand aux Amandes
Assiette de Petits Fours

COMPOTE

Compote de Rhubarbe

FRUITS

Bananes - Pommes - Poires
Raisins - Kaki - Clémentines

INFUSIONS

Café Français - Café Américain - Nescafé
Café Sanka - Maisocafé et Nescafé Décaféinés
Thé de Chine - Thé de Ceylan - Orange Pekoe
Camomille - Menthe - Tilleul - Verveine

VINS

Bordeaux Blanc - Bourgogne Blanc
Bordeaux Rouge
Ces vins, compris dans le menu,
vous seront servis sur votre simple demande.

Mercredi

CE S...
seront

T...
the ...

P A

"L

Dinner

HORS-D'ŒUVRE

Manche Butter
Green Olives - Ripe Olives - Celery in Branch
Iced Russian Caviar
Marennes Fine Oysters - Salad Caprice
Terrine of Truffled Young Pigeon
Alligator Pear à la Cubaine

SOUPS

Green Pea Veloute with Crusts
Consommé Royale
Browned Garbure Soup with Onions and Cheese

EGGS

Poached Eggs Heloïse
Shirred Eggs à la Turque

FISH

Poached Turbot Muslin Sauce
Cold Bass Génoise

ENTREE

Prime Rib of Beef Maraîchère

VEGETABLES

Hot Artichoke Oil Sauce
Fresh Spinach with Crusts
Braised Heart of Celery Demi-Glace
Risotto à l'Espagnole
Baked Idaho Potatoes - Steamed Potatoes
Potatoes Gaufrettes - Potatoes Copeaux

PASTES

Small Noodles Sicilienne

ROAST

Young Turkey with Chestnuts

FROM THE GRILL
(10 Minutes)

Broiled Saddle of Lamb on Charcoal

COLD BUFFET

York Ham - Virginia Ham with Cloves
Westphalian Ham - Parme Ham
Loin of Veal Mayonnaise - Smoked Tongue
Leg of Lamb Mint Sauce
Rack of Pork Horse Radish
Young Chicken in Jelly
Terrine of Truffled Goose Liver

SALADS

Chicory Salad with Roquefort
Heart of Romaine Salad Louisette
Marie-Stuart Salad

CHEESE

Edam Cheese - Demi-Sel - Roquefort
Selles-sur-Cher

DESSERTS

Iced Cup Monte-Cristo
Coffee Ice Cream
Custard Régence with Chocolate
Bavaroise with Nougat
Cornet with Cream and Kirsch
Friand with Almonds
Fancy Cakes

STEWED FRUIT

Stewed Rhubarb

FRUIT

Bananas - Apples - Pears
Grapes - Persimmons - Clémentine Oranges

BEVERAGES

French Coffee - American Coffee - Nescafé
Sanka Coffee - Maisocafé and Nescafé without Caffein
China Tea - Ceylon Tea - Orange Pekoe
Camomile Tea - Mint - Linden Tea - Vervain

WINES

White Bordeaux - White Burgundy
Red Bordeaux

Besides these wines - included in the meal

H. F. Alexander . . .

GALLOPING GHOST of the PACIFIC COAST

Most ships, like most people, live humble lives, enjoy a limited circle of acquaintances and pass on almost unnoticed when their day is done. Others are destined to become legendary in their own time. One such was the turbine liner which cut a racing path on two oceans under a variety of names . . . *Great Northern, Columbia, General George S. Simonds* and *H. F. Alexander*. It is difficult to say under which name she gained her greatest fame.

The *Great Northern* and her sister ship, *Northern Pacific* were turned out by the William Cramp yards at Philadelphia in 1915 for railroad-builder Jim Hill, who had earlier startled the maritime world with his giant *Minnesota* and *Dakota*. The two later ships were designed to provide coastwise express liner service between the Pacific Northwest and California, for Hill had been thwarted in his efforts to obtain rail right-of-way for this route. They would maintain schedules equal to those of competing express trains ashore.

THE SHARP-HULLED H. F. Alexander, known affectionately as the **"Galloping Ghost of the Pacific Coast,"** made record voyages on both coastwise and blue-water routes.
—JOE WILLIAMSON PHOTO

With a length of 524 feet, a 65-foot beam and moulded depth of 50 feet, the twin racers were described by those who saw them in drydock as looking "more like a carving knife on edge than a ship." Their Parsons low-pressure turbines developed 25,000 shaft horsepower, which pushed the handsome twins along at an easy 23 knots, their required delivery speed.

In Pacific Coast service, passengers could board one of the twins at Flavel (down the river from Portland, Oregon) and debark at San Francisco 24 hours later . . . *three hours faster than by the crack express trains of the day*. This service was interrupted by the first World War. *Great Northern*, with her sister-ship, was requisitioned by the Army, serving on the Atlantic where she gained fame as the fastest transport flying the American colors. In 1919, with more than 135,000 miles of trooping to her credit, much of it in fast, unconvoyed dashes across the U-boat infested Atlantic, she was taken over for Navy service as the *Columbia*.

Decommissioned in 1922, she was soon taken over by the coastwise Pacific Steamship Company as flagship of that line's California-Puget Sound fleet. She was reboilered and renamed *H. F. Alexander* after Pacific Steamship's president, and took to the West Coast service again at even higher speed. Her 1915 San Francisco-Honolulu record of three days, 18 hours, 15 minutes stood for 40 years and she had beaten the fastest troopers on the Atlantic, including the huge *Leviathan*, but now she could do 27 knots. Her clockwork schedule on the thousand-mile run between San Francisco and Seattle was 39 hours.

As automobile transportation began to make serious inroads on coastwise passenger revenues, the big "H. F." was dispatched to the East Coast during the winter months for high-speed service between New York and booming Miami. She made the New York to Florida run in 40 hours.

Even this dual service on two oceans failed to make her pay, however, and in 1936 she was laid up at Seattle, apparently permanently. Then came World War II, and the gallant old racer was transferred to the British until the United States entered the war. Then she went back to work under Army colors as the transport *General George S. Simonds*, steaming thousands of sea miles to Oran, Gibralter, Casablanca, Cape Town, Dakar and a score of other wartime ports. After her trans-Atlantic service she carried Jamacian laborers between Kingston and Norfolk.

Finally out of work again in 1946, the slim racehorse made her final voyage, back to the Philadelphia shipyard where she was born. There she was dismantled for scrap. Of the old "H. F.", legendary Galloping Ghost of the Pacific Coast, it can be truly said, "she's gone, but not forgotton".

HER CAREER FINALLY ENDED, the old **H. F. Alexander** makes her last sad voyage to the scrapyard, 1946, as the **General George S. Simonds.**

—CLARENCE N. ROGERS PHOTO

INTERIORS: Left, top to bottom: First Class Cafe, **Homeric;** First Class Library, **Queen Mary,** Chief Bos'n's Quarters, **Dominion Monarch;** Enclosed Promenade Deck, **Hanseatic.**

Above, top to bottom: Bar, **Hanseatic;** Lounge, **Italia;** Normandie Suite, **Liberte.**

Acapulco . . .

MATURE MEXICAN GLAMOUR GIRL

The conservative officials of the P & O Line would doubtless have been shocked at the launching in 1922 of their 15,043-ton *Mongolia* had they known that, at the mature age of 41 she would be flaunting herself as an all-air conditioned glamour-girl with two swimming pools, a 300-seat theater and a lido cafe deck with brightly striped awnings. Except for the fact that she was the first P & O Liner powered with steam turbines, she started life as a typical frilless working girl of that line's intermediate service. Her garb was the P & O's sober black and stone-gray of the period and the wildest entertainment to be expected aboard her was a spirited game of shuffleboard.

In 1938 she was turned over by P & O to its affiliated New Zealand Steamship Company and renamed *Rimutaka*. She served Australian and New Zealand ports under that name until 1950, when she passed to Arnold Bernstein ownership under the Italian flag and was renamed *Europa*. Shortly thereafter she hoisted the Liberian flag as the *Nassau* of Incres Steamship Company, Ltd. She was intended for cruise service to the Bahamas, but soon changed her name and flag again when she was purchased by the Mexican Government-sponsored Natumex Line (Naviera Touristica Mexicana).

Before going into service under the red, white and green tricolor as Mexico's first passenger liner, she was sent to Scotland for a major refurbishing job which, by this time, she badly needed. With the multi-million dollar face-lifting completed, her owners planned a glamorous and profitable inauguration for her . . . a plush cruise from New York to Vera Cruz, Haiti and Jamaica before dispatching her through the Panama Canal to take up her regular Los Angeles to Acapulco cruise schedule.

But as her December, 1961 sailing time approached the U.S. Coast Guard took a hand. Unimpressed by *Acapulco's* new streamlined yellow, red, green and white funnel, swimming pools, lido deck, theater, three restaurants and "world's largest floating department store," the Coast Guard forbid her sailing with passengers.

Natumex Line officials said is was just a technicality. Coast Guard spokesmen said *Acapulco* didn't meet applicable minimum safety standards, had too much wood in the cabins and other facilities below U.S. standards. The State Department got in touch with the Coast Guard and the *Acapulco* was cleared to sail on January 9, 1962, but by that time her 450 passengers had long since departed.

Since then, except for a stay, with *Dominion Monarch*, at Seattle's 1962 World's Fair, *Acapulco* has maintained the Los Angeles-Acapulco run and (at considerable cost to Mexican taxpayers) the pride of the Mexican merchant marine on the high seas.

S.S. ACAPULCO, above, is the pride of the Mexican merchant marine and that country's only major passenger liner. She's pictured below in her original guise as the P & O Lines' **Mongolia.**

THE FIRST UNITED STATES LINES' America was originally the Hamburg-American Line's **Amerika,** built at Belfast by Harland & Wolff in 1905. After serving in the first World War as a troopship, she was operated for some time in U.S. Lines all-tourist-class service, advertised as the world's largest cabin liner. In the second war she went back in government service as **the Edmund B. Alexander.** While in "nursery ship" service in 1946 she hit a floating mine in Bremer-haven harbor, but was repaired and lasted until 1957, when she was scrapped at Baltimore. Her successor, the sleek United States Lines' **America** of 1940, is pictured below.

—UNITED STATES LINES PHOTO

WASHINGTON, ABOVE, AND MANHATTAN, lower left, preceded **America** and **United States** as largest American-built liners at the time of their construction in 1932. Sister-ships of 24,289 tons, they were each driven by six steam turbines, single-reduction geared to twin screws, giving them a 21-knot service speed. **Manhattan** served in World War II as transport **Wakefield;** **Washington** as the **Mount Vernon. Manhattan** is pictured in early wartime passenger service during period of American neutrality. Large markings on her side were calculated to warn off German U-boat skippers.

—UNITED STATES LINES PHOTO

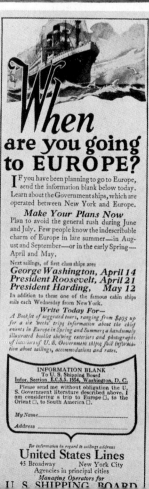

PRESIDENT GRANT, left, and President Lincoln, above, the only six-masted liners in Atlantic service, were built by Harland & Wolff at Belfast in 1907 and, at over 18,000 tons, 599 feet in length, were rated among the largest liners of their day when they went into service for Hamburg-American Line from Hamburg to New York via Boulogne and Plymouth. President Lincoln was torpedoed and sunk with the loss of 26 lives during World War I, but President Grant, renamed Republic, survived to carry Allied troops again in World War II. Laid up at the Olympia, Washington reserve fleet following the war, she's pictured below getting under way in tow of Foss Launch & Tug Company's Agness Foss and Donna Foss early in 1952. Two Moran Towing & Transportation Company tugs took her over at Panama, continuing her journey to the scrapyard.

FROM COAST TO COAST, the glamorous ocean liners depend heavily on prosaic harbor tugs to help them through the congested waters of major seaports and to their piers. Above, the 29,734-ton **Arcadia** of P & O Lines gets a hand at Seattle from units of the Foss Launch & Tug Co. fleet. Below, the French Line's **Flandre,** 20,469-ton intermediate liner, picks up her escort of Moran Towing & Transportation Co. docking tugs at completion of her 1952 maiden voyage to New York.

ELECTRONIC WATCH-KEEPER: Radar in wheel house of S.S. **America** is one of the modern navigational aids that helps make disaster at sea a rarity.

BOREDOM IS A THING OF THE PAST for liner passengers. Below, passengers on **United States** enjoy deck games, indoor pool and traditional afternoon tea served on deck by well-trained stewards.

—UNITED STATES LINES PHOTOS

BON VOYAGE: There's color and excitement at United States Lines' New York pier as departure time nears.

THERE'S MORE FUN AT SEA, TOO. Pictured below: First Class Suite and Lounge, S.S. **United States.** Lower right: Captain Frederick Fender, master of S.S. **America.**
—UNITED STATES LINES PHOTOS

NOW CARRYING first and tourist class passengers (1,228 of them at full capacity) from Montreal and Quebec to England and the Continent, the 639-foot, 21-knot turbine steamer **Homeric** is a modernized version of Matson Line's **Mariposa,** which was in pre-World War II service between San Francisco and Honolulu.

—ARCOBALENO COLORFOTO, GENOA

ISLE DE FRANCE, in her glory days as queen of the French Lines' luxury fleet, drops her gangways and prepares to leave Cherbourg for a fast westward crossing of the North Atlantic.

JUST OFF CANAL STREET, Delta Steamship Lines' luxury cruise steamer **Del Norte** is pictured at her Paydras Street Wharf moorings in her home port of New Orleans, opposite page. Huge funnels are distinguishing characteristics of **Del Norte** and her sisters **Del Mar** and **Del Sud.** Actually it's not a funnel at all, but a dummy which contains the radio and radar rooms and quarters for the operators. The oil-fired boilers exhaust through the twin black-topped stacks abaft the big funnel.

THESE THREE FINE LINERS, air-conditioned throughout and of post-war construction, offer luxury accomodations for 120 passengers, featuring the well-known 44-day cruises to east coast ports of South America. Facilities of the Delta Liners include glass enclosed promenade decks, outdoor swimming pools and sundecks, cafe and bar in addition to main dining salon, grand salon and library, electric elevators and modern shopping centers. A typical stateroom, obviously designed for the comfort and pleasure of cruise passengers, is pictured at the right.

—DELTA LINE PHOTO

THE HOME LINES GROUP'S German-flag (Hamburg Atlantic Line) turbine steamer **Hanseatic**

R.M.S. LACONIA, below, was built by Swan Hunter & Wigham Richardson at Newcastle in 1922 to replace another ship of the same name built by the same company in 1912. The first **Laconia** was torpedoed and sunk off Fastnet in 1917. The second **Laconia** was of almost the same specifications (at 601 feet she was one-foot longer), both were twin-screw ships of 16½-knot speed. The second **Laconia**, in peacetime service with her sisters **Samaria** and **Scythia** between New York, Queenstown and Liverpool, was torpedoed and sunk in World War II.

RIGHT: CAPT. CHARLES M. FORD, veteran Cunard Line officer, served as commodore of the line.

FAMOUS FLEET-MATES: In the foreground, at the Cunard Line's Piers, the second **Mauretania** and the **Queen Elizabeth** were resting briefly on this summer day in 1956. Beyond, at the United States Lines' pier are the trans-Atlantic running-mates of the American Flag company, **United States** and **America.**

——PORT OF NEW YORK AUTHORITY PHOTO

S.S. CANOPIC, below, was built in 1900 for the Dominion line as the **Commonwealth,** was transferred to White Star in 1903. Her 16-knot speed was not breath-taking, even at the turn of the century, but her owners apparently took some pride in her performance in the Boston-European service. The picture and log extract were published in 1907.

ABSTRACT OF LOG

S.S. "CANOPIC" Lieut. INMAN SEALBY, R. N. R Commander

BOSTON TO GIBRALTAR.

Left Boston L.V. Nov. 17th 1906 at 12.43 p.m.

Date	Miles	Lat.	Long.	Remarks
Nov. 18	331	42.53	63.17	moderate wind and sea
,, 19	352	42.53	55.15	overcast, dull rainy weather
,, 20	344	42.23	47.29	rough following sea,
,, 21	321	41.15	40.28	high crossed sea and squally
,, 22	344	39.45	33.11	clear weather, moderate sea
,, 23	344	37.51	26.15	fine weather, heavy s.w. swell
to Port	28			at Ponta Delgada 1.34 p.m. Nov. 23rd. left at 5.10 p.m.
,, 24	264	37.18	20.06	overcast, rainy weather. rough sea
,, 25	362	36.47	12.34	fine weather, moderate wind & sea
to Port	357			Arr at Gibraltar Nov. 26th. 1906, at 11.15 a.m.
	3047		*Total Distance*	

LAST VOYAGE: Orient Steam Navigation Company's **Orontes**, 20,186-ton turbine liner of 1926 vintage came up the Thames to Tilbury Docks on February 19, 1962, for the last time. She is dressed overall and wearing her paying-off pennant, Capt. E. G. H. Riddlesdell, R. D., R. N. R., in command. **Orontes** left her home port of London for the last time on February 26, for scrapping at Valencia, Spain.

IT HAS LONG BEEN the custom for ships of the Royal Navy to fly a paying-off pennant when ending a commission but the custom came to the Merchant Navy on September 24, 1936, when the Orient Liner **Orsova** arrived at Tilbury under command of Capt. L. F. Hubbard, R. D., R. N. R. It was her last voyage after two million sea miles and she flew a long paying-off pennant from her main mast. In 1938 the P & O Liner **Kaiser-i-Hind** came up the river flying a pennant one yard long for each year of her 24-year service.

THE PAYING-OFF PENNANT of the fine old **Orontes** was 33 yards long, representing more than three decades of brave service in war and peace.

—P & O-ORIENT LINES PHOTO

P & O CAPTAIN: Capt. Clifford Edgecombe, lower right, is veteran master of P & O-Orient Lines' service; now commands S.S. **Oriana**.

STYLE CHANGES even in the wheel houses, the nerve-centers of the ocean liners. The starkly functional wheel house of R.M.S. **Transvaal Castle**, above, is typical of the most modern design. Q.S.M.V. **Dominion Monarch**, built in 1939, displayed some of the traditional mahogony and brass of bygone days when her master, Captain G. V. Connolly turned the helm over to Seattle business man E. A. Black at the Seattle World's Fair, lower right. Classic ocean greyhound wheel house was the **Kommandohaus** of the old **Kronprinzessin Cecilie**, lower left.

DELTA LINES' American Flag liner **Del Norte,** above, leaving her home port of New Orleans on a 42-day cruise along the east coast of South America, with calls at St. Thomas, Rio, Santos, Montevideo, Buenos Aires and, on the return passage, Curacao. (Note the "Blue Peter", the blue and white code flag "P", indicating a ship is about to sail, just coming down from her forward yardarm).

—DELTA LINE PHOTO

SECTION OF BOILER ROOM, turbine R.M.S. **Transvaal Castle,** below.

—STEWART BALE PHOTO, LONDON

Opposite Page: swimming pool, **Dominion Monarch.**

Chapter Six

THE
MOTOR LINERS

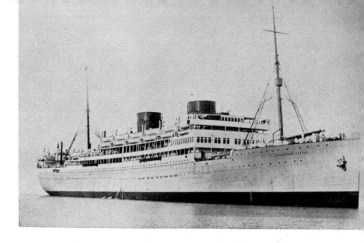

CARNARVON CASTLE, first Union - Castle motor liner. 1926.

The ocean liner has evolved through gradual stages from the first nine-knot wooden side-wheeier to the quadruple-screw giants of today driven at upwards of 40 miles an hour by turbines indirectly connected to the shafts by gears or electric drive. Steps along the way included the single-screw iron and steel vessels driven by a single triple-expansion engine, the dual-engined, twin-screw liners which ushered in the twentieth century, and the directly-connected turbine liners which closely followed them.

In all cases, the new propulsion method was tried out on medium-sized ships before it was applied to the crack liners of the period. By 1920 the diesel internal combustion engine had reached this stage in its development and there were many who were predicting that it would eventually supplant steam-driven turbines in the largest and fastest ocean liners.

Rudolph Diesel, Paris-born German inventor, made the internal combustion engine practical for marine propulsion when he developed his engine which used heavy oil rather than gasoline for fuel. As early as 1903 a small Caspian Sea coaster, the *Wandal* was in service with a primitive diesel-electric drive. The Dutch built the diesel-driven tanker *Vulcanus* in 1910. A couple of years later the Furness, Withy yard had built the first small British diesel-engined freighter and a whole fleet of small coasters with "hot bulb" heavy oil engines was being turned out at Kirkintillock, that canal port near Glasgow which gained fame as the home of "Dugan's Dew of Kirkintillock", favorite nector of Guy Gilpatrick's legendary Scots chief engineer, Glencannon of the *Inchcliff Castle*.

The first large sea-going vessel to receive diesel engines was M. S. *Selandia* of the Danish East Asiatic Company, which completed her trials early in 1912. Her 1,250-horsepower Burmeister and Wain engine drove the 370-foot, 5,000-ton freighter at a crusing speed of 11 knots. This revolutionary craft without a funnel created much interest, among her first visitors being British First Sea Lord Winston Churchill. She aroused even more interest among naval and shipping men when she completed her maiden 26,000-mile voyage without refueling and with an engineroom crew of eight men rather than the 25 required in a coal-burning steamer of similar size and cargo capacity. *Selandia* remained in service with

her original engine until 1939, covering well over a million sea miles with less than two weeks total time off for engine repairs.

The building of diesel-driven ships was halted by the first World War. There was no time to waste on new-fangled machinery and the yards concentrated on ships powered by simple, standardized reciprocating steam engines. However the diesel received its trial by battle in the submarines of all the maritime powers, so its improvement and development was not halted entirely.

The motorship figured prominently in post-war shipbuilding, with the *Aorangi* of the Union Steamship Company of New Zealand in service in 1924 as the first motorship to qualify as a first-class passenger liner. The quadruple screw *Aorangi* was 600 feet in length with a gross tonnage of 23,000. Her four direct-drive Fairfield-Sulzer engines developed a combined 13,000 horsepower to provide her with an 18-knot top speed. On her long-haul service from Sydney to Vancouver via .New Zealand, the Fiji Islands and Honolulu she carried enough fuel oil for her own round-trip voyage, plus enough extra to bunker her steam-driven consort in the Canadian service. Like the pioneer *Selandia*, *Aorangi* served long and well, finally retiring in 1953 when the Union Steam trans-Pacific service was discontinued.

A year after the *Aorangi* on the Pacific came the first trans-Atlantic motor liner, Swedish-American Line's first *Gripsholm*. A twin-screw ship of 23,600 tons, 574 feet in length, her two Burmeister and Wayne engines developed 13,500 horsepower; gave her a sea speed of 17 knots.

Gripsholm and her later fleet-mate, Swedish-American's first *Kungsholm*, were highly successful ships and other passenger lines soon let contracts for motor liners of gradually increasing length and tonnage. The French Line's first diesel-driven passenger ship was *LaFayette,* a 603-foot quadruple-screw cabin liner turned out by the Penhoet yards of St. Nazaire. (She was destroyed by fire while in drydock in 1938). The Royal Mail Steam Packet Company took delivery from Harland and Wolff of the handsome 630-foot twin-screw motor liners *Asturias* and *Alcantara* and the Union-Castle Mail Steamship Company placed its first motor liner, *Carnarvon Castle* in intermediate service in 1926. She did so well that she was followed by a whole fleet of diesel-driven *Castle* liners, for the economical diesel engine was at its best on the long mail run from Southampton to Cape Town.

The venerable Bibby Line, famous for its tall-stacked trooping liners which carried British forces to India and the Eastern fronts in four wars, had two motor liners in service as early as 1920, *Dorsetshire* and *Somersetshire.* By the outbreak of World War II there was only one steamer left in the Bibby fleet, but you couldn't tell by looking at the ships. The motorized *Shires* were carefully designed to look exactly like the classic troopers · of old, tall, raked pink funnels, multiple lofty masts and all. It had been assumed that *Selandia* had set the pattern for motorships and that the funnel would soon vanish from the seas, but such was not the case. Tradition required at least one funnel painted in the company colors for identification if not esthetic reasons.

Most motorship designers compromised with shorter, fatter stacks than the tall raked funnels required for adequate draft and soot removal on the coal-burning steamers, but as oil-fired steamers became more common their stacks were shortened and fattened also and it became more and more difficult to distinguish a motor liner from a steamer.

By 1927 it was beginning to appear that the predictions of diesel-driven liners in the highest speed and luxury class were accurate. The Italian Line's first M. S. *Augustus* of that years was over seven hundred feet in length with a gross tonnage of 30,400. Built at Genoa by the Ansaldo yards, as was the great Italian Blue Riband-holder *Rex, Augustus* had accommodations for 2,500 passengers and a crew of 450. Her four propellers driven by four 7,000-horse-power M. A. N.-Savoia diesels gave her a sea speed of 21 knots . . . not record-winning speed, but moving in that direction.

In 1930 and 1931 the British White Star Line took delivery of a pair of twin-screw motor liners, *Britannic* and *Georgic,* from Harland and Wolff. These big cabin class liners of 26,900 and 27,800 tons respectively were not quite as large as the *Augustus,* but in length (712 feet) they marked the high tide of big motor liner construction.

Other large motor liners followed *Augustus, Britannic* and *Georgic,* notably Union- Castle Line's *Capetown Castle* of 1937 and Shaw-Savill's *Dominion Monarch* of 1939, both big, luxurious ships designed for long-voyage comfort on the runs to Capetown and beyond to the Antipodes.

It is significant that all but one of these ships, *Augustus, Britannic, Georgic, Capetown Castle* and *Dominion Monarch* . . . the largest motor liners ever built, are out of service as this is written and that no new construction of equal size has replaced them. The Scandinavian trans-Atlantic lines and the Italian Line are notable operators of motor liners in the post-World War II period, but none of their new ships are as large as the biggest pre-war motor liners. Union-Castle and Shaw-Savill, whose long-haul services seemed made to order for motorships have, in recent years, returned to the steam turbine for the porpulsion of their prestige liners.

There are no present indications that the diesel engine will replace steam turbines in the enginerooms of the ultra-large, ultra-fast ocean greyhounds of the future. The coming of the American nuclear-powered cargo-passenger liner *Savannah,* her turbines powered by atomically-generated steam, makes such a development even more doubtful. However, the invention of Dr. Diesel seems to have found a firm place at sea in the propulsion of ocean liners of moderate size and speed. From all indications it is a field in which it will remain for many years to come.

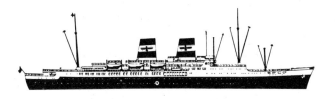

THE QUADRUPLE-SCREW motor liner **Aorangi** which served joint CPR-Union Steamship Company Canadian-Australasian service between Canada, Australia and New Zealand both before and after the second World War, was the first big liner with diesel engines. She was built by Fairfield at Glasgow in 1924.

—JOE WILLIAMSON PHOTO

NOORDAM, trim Holland-American cargo- passenger motor liner, gets an assist from Moran Towing & Transportation Company's **Moira Moran.**

THE FIRST AUGUSTUS of the Italian Line, built in Italy in 1927 was, at 30,400 tons, the largest motor liner ever built.

—ITALIAN LINE PHOTO

FOURTH HOLLAND-AMERICA LINER to bear the name, the latest **Statendam** figured in a unique christening ceremony on January 23, 1957, when Princess Beatrix, eighteen-year-old heiress apparent to the Netherlands Throne poured a glass of champagne over the ship's 300-pound bell in the flower-decked dining salon. With an overall length of 642 feet and a gross tonnage of 24,294, **Statendam** is a fine example of the luxurious intermediate liners of today.

—HOLLAND-AMERICAN LINE PHOTO

SWEDISH-AMERICAN LINE'S first motor liner **Kungsholm** is pictured above in the harbor of Gothenburg, Sweden. Built in 1928 by Blohm & Voss at Hamburg to replace the line's first **Kungsholm,** (a steamer of 1902 vintage scrapped that year), her tremendous success did much to popularize diesel propulsion for passenger liners in the late 1920's and 30's. During World War II she served the United States as the transport **John Ericsson,** has since been completely rebuilt as Home Lines' **Italia** (opposite page).

GRIPSHOLM, pictured below in World War II service, was the first Atlantic liner with diesel engines. Built in 1925 by Armstrong, Whitworth & Co., Newcastle-on-Tyne, she gained fame as a repatriation ship during the war afterward reestablishing North German Lloyd post-war Atlantic service as the **Berlin.**

—SWEDISH-AMERICAN LINE PHOTO

RIGHT: CAPT. D. W. SORRELL, Cunard Line master, at docking telegraph of Cunard-White Star motor liner **Britannic.**
—CUNARD LINE PHOTO

WITH HER SISTER-SHIP GRIPSHOLM, M.S. **Kungsholm** was one of the first large trans-Atlantic motor liners. She's pictured here as Home Line's **Italia,** having made her maiden voyage under that flag in June, 1949. Late in 1960, the luxuriously refurbished veteran was withdrawn from trans-Atlantic service to establish weekly seven-day cruise service between New York and Nassau. Long known as the "Hostess of the Atlantic," this friendly, comfortable ship has earned a similar reputation in cruise service.

—HOME LINES PHOTO

FLANDRE, French Line intermediate liner, docking at New York.

CAPETOWN CASTLE, above, was Union-Castle Line's largest motor liner.

ITALIAN LINE'S M.S. VULCANIA gets under way from New York pier to begin voyage of July 10, 1958 (below). Crowd at United States Line pier in the background, indicates that S.S. **United States,** with the engineers pouring the fuel oil to her forward boilers, will soon be following **Vulcania.**

CUNARD-WHITE STAR MOTOR LINER BRITANNIC was the last ship to carry White Star colors on the Atlantic.

BRITANNIC'S SISTER-SHIP, GEORGIC, shown at the right as a British trooper, lost one of her twin funnels in later years, somewhat spoiling her good looks.

Q.S.M.V. **DOMINION MONARCH** on maiden voyage, 1939.

THE DOMINION MONARCH IS SHOWN at sea, left, and moored at Seattle in 1962 as a hotel ship for the World's Fair. While at Seattle, a pilot film for a new television series was filmed aboard her and efforts were made to lease her for several years to serve as a floating "set" for ocean liner films. The Shaw Savill Line refused to permit such use, however, and early in 1963 this splendid motor liner crossed the Pacific under her own power for scrapping in Japan.

CAPTAIN K. D. G. FISHER, lower right, Commodore of the Shaw Savill Line, commanded **Dominion Monarch** during her final service as the line's flagship.

THE WORLD'S TEN LARGEST MOTOR LINERS

	Name	Tonnage	Company	Date Built	Flag
1.	Augustus	32,650	Italian Line	1927	Italian
2.	Roma	32,583	Italian Line	1926	Italian
3.	Georgic	27,759	White Star	1932	British
4.	Dominion Monarch°	27,155	Shaw Savill	1939	British
5.	Augustus°	27,090	Italian Line	1952	Italian
6.	Giulio Cesare°	27,078	Italian Line	1951	Italian
7.	Capetown Castle°	27,072	Union-Castle	1937	British
8.	Britannic	26,840	White Star	1930	British
9.	Athlone Castle°	25,567	Union-Castle	1935	British
10.	Stirling Castle°	25,554	Union-Castle	1936	British

*In service as of January, 1962.

Dinner Adieu
Wednesday, April 18, 1962

Farewell Dominion Monarch

Soon:-
She will be gone,
but not forgotten.
Remembered in Peace and War
and gracious to the end.

Happy To Meet - Sorry To Part -
Happy To Meet Again!

Chief Steward:
G. Goodman

Chef:
J. J. Farrell

MENU

Chilled Fruit Juice
Grapefruit Cocktail

Liver Sausage   Egg & Tomato Mayonnaise   Tunnyfish
Pickled Red Cabbage   Sardines in Oil   Artichokes Vinaigret

Consomme Colbert   Cream of Tomato

Fillets of Cod, Mornay
Grilled Salmon Steak, Parsley Butter

Braised Celery Hearts
Chicken & Ham Vol-au-Vents

To Order: Fried Crumbed Pork Cutlet, Pineapple

Roast Sirloin of Beef, Sweetcorn Fritters
Roast Norfolk Duck, English Style

Buttered Carrot Rounds   Brussels Sprouts

Potatoes: Roast   Boiled   Creamed

Cold: York Ham   Roast Pork
Roast Lamb   Rolled Ox Tongue

Salads: Plain   Macedoine

Dressings: French   Mayonnaise   Apple Sauce
English Plum Pudding, Rum Sauce   Raspberry Jellies
Cream Buns   Peach Melba

Canape Diane

Dessert

YOU NEVER KNOW WHERE THEY'LL TURN UP NEXT: Old ocean liners, it sometimes seems, never die, but change their flags and names and keep on working. Above is S.S. **Iroquois** as she looked when new in 1927, an East Coast liner of Clyde Lines. (She worked the Pacific Coast too, for a short time, as running-mate to **Yale** on the Los Angeles-San Diego-San Francisco run.) At the right you see her as she looks now as **Ankara** of Turkish State Lines, following a brief tour of duty as the hospital ship **Solace.** Built at Newport News, the 6,178-ton liner is driven by four steam turbines.

—MORAN TOW LINE

FAREWELL TRIBUTE to the "Old D.M.," a prime favorite among travellers to Australia and New Zealand, was the verse written by Miss Georgiana Williamson, secretary to Southampton's globe-trotting ex-mayor Hector Young, and reproduced on the farewell menu above. When the old flagship sailed from Perth on her final voyage all the lights of the city were turned on in her honor, as they had been for Colonel John Glenn on his first American orbital flight a few weeks earlier.

SEA QUEEN OF THE NETHERLANDS

ABOVE: Nieuw Amsterdam as troop transport.

BELOW: Nieuw Amsterdam in Peacetime service.

APRIL 10, 1946 WAS A DAY to be remembered in the proud little kingdom of Holland. That was the day **Nieuw Amsterdam** came home from the wars. For bomb-battered Rotterdam it symbolized, perhaps more than anything since the Canadians rolled into town after the German surrender, the fact that they were free and that the Netherlands had played her role and played it well.

Nieuw Amsterdam, 36,287-ton flagship of Holland-America Line and largest vessel in the Netherlands merchant marine, was between La Guaira and Porto Cabello, Venezuela, on a West Indies cruise when World War II hit Holland. Commodore Johannes J. Bijl turned the ship and steamed for New York. As she docked at Hoboken word came of the Nazi bombing of defenseless Rotterdam.

After a refit as a trooper at Todd's Brooklyn yards, **Nieuw Amsterdam** set out to help the Allies win the war at sea.

It was six years and seven months before the people of Holland saw her again. In that time she had steamed a half-million miles and transported nearly that many troops to the battlefields of the world.

It was on the ninth anniversary of her launching that she came home again, still sombre in rust-streaked gray war paint, but with her two huge funnels freshly painted in the green, white and buff colors of the Holland-America Line and the city of Rotterdam, and with all her signal flags flying. She came out of a curtain of black storm clouds, her deep siren booming, and the people of Holland laughed and wept to see her come. No ship has received a greater ovation. From sea to port the riverbanks were black with children waving the Dutch tricolor and dense crowds jammed the waterfront.

As the great ship swung round toward her old pier the sun broke through and the band struck up **Wilhelmus,** the national anthem. It was a day to be remembered in Holland.

Nieuw Amsterdam is back again in the trans-Atlantic service now. Although the new **Rotterdam** has supplanted her as flagship of the fleet she's still a brave and beautiful ship, one of the loveliest liners ever built.

And to the people of Holland, whose pride she is, no ship, however grand, will ever supplant her as the Sea Queen of the Netherlands.

SPLENDID NEW FLAGSHIP of Home Lines, the 34,000-ton **Oceanic** was launched at Monfalcone, Italy on January 15, 1963; will enter Canada-European service in 1964. A true luxury liner, her facilities include two swimming pools, closed-circuit television, chapel, cinemascope theater, children's and teen-agers' public rooms and complete air conditioning. Her 61,000-horsepower turbines are expected to give her a speed of 27 knots. Other photos show interiors of older Home Liners **Italia** and **Hanseatic.**

—HOME LINES PHOTOS

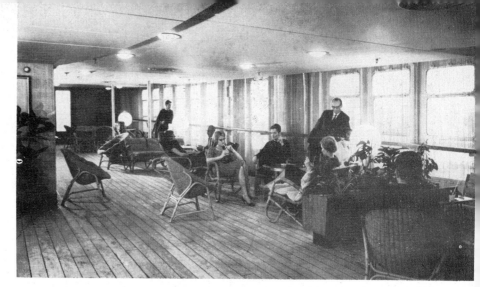

HOME LINE CAPTAINS: Admiral Constantine C. Condoyannis, left, retired as Greek Naval flag officer in 1948 to assume command of Home Liner **Atlantic.** Captain Eugen Strinz, below, a native of Luebeck, Germany, was cadet on square-rigged schoolship **Prinz Eitel Friedrich;** served as Hamburg American Line officer before becoming master of **Hanseatic.**

—MORAN TOWING & TRANSPORTATION CO., INC. PHOTO

UNITED STATES LINES Commodore John W. Anderson on bridge of **United States.**
—UNITED STATES LINES PHOTO

CUNARD LINE Commodore Donald Mac Lean, D.S.C., R.N.R.
—CUNARD LINE PHOTO BY GEORGE V. BIGELOW

COMMODORE A. G. PATEY, Union - Castle Mail Steamship Co., Ltd.
—TERENCE J. MCNALLY PHOTO, CAPE TOWN

COMMODORE L. J. HOPKINS, Shaw Savill Line.

COMMODORE CORNELIS G. KOOYMAN,
Holland-America Line.

COMMODORE L. A. HILL, P & O-Orient Lines.
—CUNARD LINE PHOTOS

CUNARD LINE Commodore Morris on bridge
of **Queen Elizabeth,** October, 1958.
—CUNARD LINE PHOTO BY W. A. PROBST

COMMODORE H. J. EHMAN, American President Lines.

R.M.S. TRANSVAAL CASTLE

GOLDEN ROOM, Transvaal Castle, above, overlooks Lido and pool areas. Design by Jon Bannenberg, based on ancient Persian motif.

FIRST CLASS CARD ROOM, Windsor Castle, below, is circular tent-shaped room in gray and Chinese yellow. Corona of star lights crowns brass "tent pole."

GLEAMING ELECTRIC GALLEY of Transvaal Castle, below, keeps 728 passengers happy on long voyage to South Africa.

S.S. FRANCE

FIRST CLASS DINING SALON of S.S. France, above, is entered by central grand staircase. Decor by Mme. Darbois-Gaudin is accented by lacquered panels of M. Jean Mandaroux on the theme "The Pleasures of Life."

DINING SALON of Liberte, below, shows changing style in French Line interior decor.
—FRENCH LINE PHOTOS

FIRST CLASS LIBRARY, S.S. France, above, is circular room designed by Jean Leleu, contains 2,000 books bound in coded colors to indicate language of text.

GRAND SALON of France, below, is a huge room, the dance floor alone covering 1,000 square feet, but decorator Maxime Old has preserved an intimate atmosphere on its fringes.

FINAL VOYAGE, Dominion Monarch

—PHOTO BY ALBERT N. PLUSH

THE END